PRAISE FOR THE AUTHOR

"I have been working with Sharon Jurd for the past 7 and half years she has helped me implement all of my systems and processes into my businesses. Together we have increased my customer service satisfaction and ensured my customers kept coming back. Sharon helped me to confidently take time out of my business and travel to Europe and other countries for two years which I have now successfully fulfilled my life goal. I will not own a business without having Sharon working with me."

Michael Wilson
Entrepreneur and Business Owner

"It's one thing to become a Salesperson ranking in the Top 2% of a Global Franchise..... then become a franchisor in an unrelated field and bring on 13 franchisees in the first 12 months. Sharon Jurd is one of those people that make things happen.

Sharon doesn't use magic tricks or high pressure sales, she's about being structured, putting processes in place to make your business work, being committed to and passionate about what you do.

If the words determined, persistent, organised and disciplined relate to you, or if you think they should, this is a lady you need to listen to."

Marcus Kroek
Business and Executive Coach
ActionCOACH

"I have had the pleasure of being invited to speak at a Sharon Jurd Event. Sharon organised this event with the utmost professionalism and caring about the attendees. Knowing what the attendees wanted Sharon organised the correct type of speakers to benefit them fully. This event was one of the best seminars I have attended either as a speaker or a guest."

Janet Culpitt
Director
Arrow Insurance
Wealth Creation & Protection

PRAISE FOR THE AUTHOR

"We had been running our own businesses for almost thirty years when we met Sharon Jurd. Our customers loved us - we knew what they wanted, and we made sure they got it. The only problem was that we hated our life. We had an impossibly chaotic workload, lousy cashflow, and no way out.

It wasn't an overnight transformation, and it's not rocket science, but from the day Sharon started coaching us, things started to change. Sharon's real-world business skills and experience gave us the confidence to trust her advice, and in the same way that a coach improves the performance of an athlete, Sharon helped us focus on the right things. Slowly but surely we tamed the chaos with clearer priorities and better systems, and one day at a time we're getting our life back. Thanks Sharon!"

Rowan & Lea Pettett
Directors
Technopronto
Simpler, Smarter, Faster IT

"Working with Sharon has changed my business beyond belief and my motivation to grow my business is now greater than ever. Sharon's simple systems allow me the freedom to do the things I enjoy in my business and life. Sharon has shown me that my new found consistency brings great rewards. I have never been more positive about my business and personal future."

Elisa Rooney & Peter Korzuch
Directors
Jazz Cleaning
One Stop Cleaning Service

HOW TO GROW YOUR
BUSINESS
FASTER THAN YOUR COMPETITOR

The Secrets to Freedom & Success in 5 easy steps

GLOBAL
PUBLISHING
G R O U P

Global Publishing Group
Australia • New Zealand • Singapore • America • London

HOW TO GROW YOUR
BUSINESS
FASTER THAN YOUR COMPETITOR

The Secrets to Freedom
& Success in 5 easy steps

SHARON JURD

First Edition 2013

National Library of Australia
Cataloguing-in-Publication entry:

Jurd, Sharon, author.

How to grow your business faster than your competitor: the secrets to freedom & success in 5 easy steps / Sharon Jurd.

1st ed.
ISBN: 9781922118219 (paperback)

Success in business.
Creative ability in business.

650.1

Published by Global Publishing Group
PO Box 517 Mt Evelyn, Victoria 3796 Australia
Email info@TheGlobalPublishingGroup.com

For Further information about orders:
Phone: +61 3 9736 1156 or Fax +61 3 8648 6871

I dedicate this book to all of the people who have allowed me to be a part of their business and their life. You took the 'plunge' and trusted me, sometimes with your greatest asset or life savings. You knew all the answers all along; together, we could achieve your goals at a greater level.

Sharon Jurd

ACKNOWLEDGEMENTS

Every person that is in my life has given me part of them. This has made me the person I am today. I would like to thank you all.

My Mum and Dad, Kevin and Wendy George, have been together forever and have given me everything I need to be a good person. I always know I am loved. My two sisters, Sonya Moore and Kylie George, we like to think we are nothing alike but in fact we are exactly the same. I love knowing that I can call my family and they will always be there for me, no matter how far away I am.

My children, Jacob and Casey Jurd, you are always in my heart and thoughts. I have never been more in love. I am so proud of you.

My closest friend, Nicole Clarke, who is the only one awake at 4am to talk to me on the phone for hours on end. Michael Wilson who I mentored but who eventually became my mentor, reminds me of everything I once told him when I question myself; thank goodness for Face Time!

In business I have a number of mentors who have helped me form my perspective on what makes a great leader, mentor and business owner; Charles Tarbey who has taught me about the importance of relationships, growing a great business and franchising; my friend Pat Mesiti whom I met many moons ago and is a positive motivator in my life and my business - thanks for reminding me how brilliant I am; Brad Sugars who showed me that businesses can grow fast through simple structure and process; Marcus Kroek who has coached me for so long through different phases, I love that he can tell me how it really is - no fluffing around. Thank you to Darren Stephens who showed me a way of getting my dream of writing a book to become a reality. I would also love to say thank you to Helen Busse from Global Publishing for all of your time, effort and support – it didn't go unnoticed.

To my partner in life and business, John Sanders, being together makes my life just right. Who would have thought…I love that we can be business partners and still be friends. Thank you for cooking dinner for me on so many nights…I love you! xx

To help you Grow Your Business Fast I have included a Bonus Offer of a further 7 top tips from myself and 6 other successful business people.

These tips will help you to reach your goals and give you important information crucial to people who are in business for themselves!

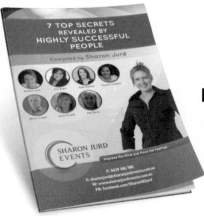

Special Report
(Valued at $97.00)

"7 Top Secrets Revealed By Highly Successful People"

To Access This FREE Report Simply Go To www.SharonJurdEvents.com.au And Download It.

TABLE OF CONTENTS

FOREWORD

People go into business for themselves for a myriad of reasons. Some are looking to make more money. Others are looking for more time; still others, more freedom. Heck, some people are just sick and tired of doing something for someone else they could be doing for themselves, by themselves.

Every person who starts a business has at least one goal in mind, which is <u>not to fail</u>, (this in itself is part of the challenge, but more on that later)

The reason so many startup and early stage entrepreneurs focus on the goal of "not failing" is because they aren't always certain what it takes to succeed.

The question our focus and energy should be concentrated on answering is, "What does it take to succeed in business—my business? "

What does it take?

Imagination? You bet; it's the fuel for the dream of working for yourself rather than plying your time, talents, and energy for someone else in an enterprise you'll never own. Your dream moves from possibility toward reality when motivation kicks in and you transform from an idea to initiation an action and the journey begins.

Filled with fantasies of instant success and bold and bodacious plans of never having to look back, sooner or later, something pretty predictable happens to most of us—doubt begins to seep into our thoughts and dampens our unbridled optimism.

Luckily, determination kicks in and through concreted commitment, force of will, and strength of spirit we pursue our business dream. For some it's enough, for others no matter how hard they work, how many hours in a day they dedicate they're on a path to a destination other than they intended—less time, less freedom, less money, and a boatload of uncertainty.

Alas! There's hope!! What separates the few from the many when it comes to succeeding in business isn't luck, although it's nice when it happens. It isn't deep pockets--big budgets often hide huge errs of judgment and even near-fatal flaws. Even a new product, a unique service, or a novel approach to an existing industry won't guarantee our success forever.

Nope, the critical element in creating initial and lasting success is systemization. It's THE distinction that makes the difference between having a business you own and a business that owns you.

Systemization is what allows you to sustain your business. It's what allows you to scale as you go. It's what enables you to create predictable results and lasting success.

Systemizing your time, energy, efforts, resources, and yes, even your relationships can be a game-changer. Knowing what to do first, second, and so on is what enables us not only to be efficient, but also to be effective. Systemization separates the success inhibitors from the success accelerators.

I know, you're probably saying to yourself—"that's all grand and glorious, but what if I don't know the system I should be using?" Great question and I'm glad you asked.

If each and every one of us had to figure our how to succeed in business through trial and error, we'd all pretty much be doomed to failure. Fortunately, we don't need to "discover" the system for ourselves or by ourselves, we need only to look around and find the formulas that work for others.

In many cases, we can look at other businesses in our industry and search for clues there. Better yet, we can look at an industry of systematic business growth like franchises.

Still there is a single best option for determining what YOU need to be doing right NOW in your business. Find a mentor, a coach, an expert teacher, trainer, consultant, or expert "who has been there and done that"—exactly what you're trying to do--maximize your wins and minimize your mistakes.

Seek out and source a trusted resource to guide, support, and show you how to focus on the highest and best use of your time and to leverage every asset and resource at your disposal and then some.

No, I'm not saying you run down to "the consultant store" and buy you a shiny new "advisor" right off the shelf. What I am saying is access to expertise is all around you—on the internet, in audios, podcasts, webinars, seminars, blogs, and yes—BOOKS!

In your hands you hold the key to a chest of unlocked treasure. In this very book you can find the levers to elevate your business potential and escalate your profits. Sharon Jurd, is one of those "been there done that" experts. Not a self-proclaimed business genius or guru but a real world, hands-on, no B.S. author, expert, mentor, and yes, successful business owner.

Sharon's been punched in the gut by bad luck and personal adversity she had to overcome, not just once but on multiple occasions. She had to learn the hard way, you get to learn "the lucky way". As Seneca the Roman Philosopher, Politician, and Stoic said, "Luck is what happens when preparation meets opportunity."

Here is the opportunity, are you prepared to seize it?

I believe you are.

Take ethical advantage of Sharon's experience—learn from it, model it, grow from it, and earn from it. Her success can be your success and will be your great fortune for having found Sharon and her book.

As Sharon shares in her book with you, systems are the nervous system and skeletal structure, which your business survival, success, sustainability and scalability depend.

She'll help you consciously discover or uncover "the WHY of your business". Sharon will help you examine and meticulously craft your story of what powers and propels you to be an extraordinary business owner and an owner of an exceedingly exceptional business.

This book, her book will help you shatter the barriers that have held you back and move forward with a profound confidence in knowing there's a blueprint and a framework for creating predicable, replicable success in your business AND in your life.

You'll learn how to position yourself as the "obvious expert' and "the only viable solution" by promoting yourself, your business, product, or service in a uniquely valuable and viable way.

Strategies in this book will help you discover how to recognize and regard your personal and professional relationships as the jewels and gems they are—priceless, precious assets no one can succeed without.

Sharon Jurd will guide you, inspire you, challenge you and show you how to grow your business faster (and better) than your competitors in 5 Easy Steps.

A final note, and it's incredibly important... yes the steps are easy <u>but the like</u> on any journey, the steps don't take themselves. You have to embrace the opportunity and envision your destination, and get your feet moving toward a better, more certain, and prosperous future.

Like all great journeys that result in memorable achievement you need a goal, a map, a guide, and the tools to sustain you along the way. This book gives you everything you need to get from where you are to where you want to go.

With a simple, single, but not a solitary step, the journey begins...turn the page and prosper.

To Your Success,

Spike Humer
Bestselling Author and Entrepreneurial Business Growth Expert

INTRODUCTION

I was 29 years of age, married with two small children Jacob aged four and Casey aged two. My work life balance was perfect and life overall was great, I was happy. What I didn't know was that it was all about to change.

It was the 30th of June and I woke up with another headache. My simple remedy was to take some pain relieving medication. I never gave it a thought that popping pain killers had become a daily ritual over the previous couple of weeks. I had been experiencing some blurry vision and had made an appointment and visited my eye specialist the previous week. Having had my eyes lasered the previous year I was concerned that I was having some side effects from my eye operation. After extensive testing he assured me my eyesight was perfect and whatever was causing the blurry vision definitely wasn't my eyes. I didn't realise at the time that this blurry vision seemed to coincide with my headaches.

My husband at the time, an interstate truck driver, was at home which was unusual, so I left my children with him so I could do my grocery shopping. Whilst out shopping my head started to ache again and the blurry vision was back. It got so bad that I didn't finish my shopping but headed for home. I lived about 7 Kilometres from town. During the trip home I stopped twice to try and wait for my vision to clear. I thought that this must be what a migraine is like. My mother suffered from migraines at times when I was younger and now I was appreciating how bad they must have been. I made it home and went to bed with the good old tried and tested wet washer on my forehead.

Later that day my sister Kylie came by on her way to my parents' house another 15 minutes out of town. She suggested that as my husband was about to leave, I should go with her to my parents' home where Mum would feed and bath my two children and then I could come back home, put them straight to bed and not have to worry. I agreed if I didn't have to drive. I arrived at my parents' house and Mum and Kylie took my children inside. I walked in holding my forehead and immediately lay down on the couch saying hello to my Dad on the way in. Within a minute or two of lying on the couch I felt unusual. I can't quite describe it but I knew it wasn't normal. I got up off the couch announcing to my father that I didn't feel well and then I collapsed. Little did I know I had a stroke! After an unknown time frame I became semi-conscious and was immediately aware that I could not talk and could not move parts of my body. I didn't know where I was and wasn't familiar with my surroundings or the people around me. The next 24 hours was a blur. I had another small secondary stroke during the next night. Things were happening around me that I did not understand. What I did realise though was that I was no longer in control.

Until this very moment I had felt I was in control of everything around me.

Until this very moment I had felt I was in control of everything around me. It now appeared that I was not. My life was, to me, crumbling down around me. My speech was impaired so communication was difficult. I had no mobility down one side of my body and could not function independently. It became apparent that my husband didn't know where my daughter went to day care and while he knew the school my son went to he wasn't sure where to drop him or at what times. My normal routine was not known to any of my family or friends in any great detail. It's not that my husband was a bad father; it was the fact that I had structured my life around me as I was the nucleus for the success of my business and life. Once I was removed from it, my life could not function correctly. We had a business to run and children to look after and little did I know at that time, it was going to be a further 12 months before I was capable of returning to 'normal.'

Over the coming months I had to concentrate on my recovery, I had no choice but to focus on my health. I had to rely greatly on people around me for major support. People around me were doing everything they possibly could without knowing what had to be done. My daily life was usually very busy and there was no way for my support network to know what had to be dealt with until something became evident to them, usually by way of urgency or drama. How they coped I do not know and I am really grateful for their help and support.

During this period I not only learnt how to walk, talk and feed myself again, I had to discover a whole new way of controlling my life. This event in my life totally transformed the way I live and work. I never wanted my life or my business to be out of control ever again.

My recovery was outstanding; as I improved physically and mentally I started to put some simple strategies into my life and business. Using simple systems, I wanted to have control even when I wasn't there to be in control. I wanted my family and business to grow and thrive even in turbulent times. Later on when I opened a new start-up business I realised that I needed it to grow. It could not be in the start-up phase for too long; the younger it was the more vulnerable it would be if I was ever to become incapacitated again.

My systems developed more and more. They were proving to be successful. Time after time my systems helped grow my businesses fast, allowed me to be in control and never allowed for chaos at home or at work. Soon I had other business owners wanting to know what I was doing. My competitors were worried, running scared in fact. I was asked, "How can you do so much in your day?" "How do you get everything done?" "You seem to be everywhere!" "You must be superwoman!" Well no, I am not superwoman but I am self disciplined at following a few easy steps every day. By doing this, it appears that I achieve the unachievable. I have never had so much time to travel and spend with family and friends. I now have the money to choose when and where I want to eat out for dinner. The life that I always wanted is now here.

I have used these simple steps in the variety of businesses that I have owned or through my coaching clients businesses. Have they been tested? Yes! I had another stroke 9 years later and the outcome was a very different one. This time my life and businesses did not get out of control and my income and profitability remained stable. I was confident that I was in control and my recovery was so much quicker. I must admit though, that I will not be using my health to test it again.

If you want to overcome chaos in your business and live the life you have always wished for, spend some time with me by reading this book, follow my steps and you too can achieve the unachievable.

Grab a highlighter, marker or pen and mark important notes throughout this book so you can come back, refresh and take action. I have included examples and questions in each chapter for you to complete and implement in your business immediately. Each small step you take leads to a big result. The first step is to keep reading and don't stop growing!

> *Now is the absolute right time.*
>
> *Sharon Jurd*

CHAPTER 1

Why Your Own Business?

Sometimes your only available transportation is a leap of faith.

Margaret Shepard

CHAPTER 1

Why your own Business?

Before we get too far into this book we need to take a step back for just a little while. We all have a reason why we wanted to start our business. I surely had mine. I was working in a real estate office as the manager. I had a boss who, over time, trusted me enough to leave me alone to manage and grow the business; just how I liked it. In fact, I had the 'perfect' job. I was paid well and was appreciated. The business grew from a small independent office with two staff members to a franchised office with an average of 13 staff at any time. The business turnover and market share grew dramatically. I had fantastic communication with my boss. We talked about what the business was achieving and where we were headed. I grew that business like it was my own, but it wasn't.

One day I looked at his children and thought what a wonderful business he had built for them so they could have such a great life. That's when the penny dropped for me. I looked at my two children and thought, what am I building for my children? Yes, I was paid well and could use that money to invest and build a great life for them but then I asked myself the question, how secure was my job? His children would soon, possibly, want to take over the business and rightly so. Where did that leave me? My boss assured me there was always going to be a place for me there, he even offered me more money but his words (and money) were not enough for my children's future. In my own mind I always thought I would buy into this business but my boss told me that was never going to be. I realised I had to go and do it for myself. Yes, I was going to go and own my own real estate office and grow a future for myself and my family.

> *The pictures in my head weren't of failure but success.*

The very next moment, along came the self doubt. Am I a raving lunatic? What if it fails? There will be no future for my family. I would have to contemplate moving my family to another town, new schools and new friends. What was I thinking? But my self belief kept getting stronger and stronger. The pictures in my head weren't of failure but success. I didn't see the hard times I was about to endure but the benefits of reward that would come my way from my hard work and experience. I could see the business not as a small business but one that was going to conquer the world! I would have the best real estate office ever! I could see the neon sign with my name up in lights already. My family and friends were saying to me, "If you are successfully doing it for someone else now you can do it for yourself." Of course they were right, I was good at what I was doing so how could it not be successful? The thoughts of starting my own business would not go away and it became all too consuming but still I made no real commitment to do it until I met with a man whom I knew very little about, for coffee. What I knew about him was that I had great respect for what he had to say.

Little did I know he was going to say something to me over coffee that day that I would never forget. He asked me, "Why are you putting off owning an office?" I replied with something embarrassing like, "I don't know" and this is when my life changed. He said to me, "At the moment it seems like this is the biggest decision you will ever make, but it will be the smallest. Next minute you will be making decisions about a second office or a third office and then at that time they will seem like the biggest decisions you have ever made. You see when you look back on a decision you realise you will always be making a bigger one than the last. When you make the decision the weight of the world will be off your shoulders." I can't remember my reply; it must have also been trivial. What I do remember is the emotion those words brought to me. It made sense somehow. So I went out and took the weight off my shoulders and made the smallest decision of my life.

Just as a side note, the other thing I did not know that day was that four years later that man was to become my life partner, now that was a bigger decision. To all of you guys out there, I do not suggest this as your next pick up line at the night club by the way.

Not everyone's story is like mine and mine is probably not typical. Owning your own business comes about in many different ways, what's your story? Everyone has one. Some people I have spoken to have bought an existing business from their current boss or even just came across a business opportunity almost by chance. It doesn't matter how you came across the business it's about why? A lot of my clients tell me that it just came simply from frustration. They were working hard, not earning a lot of money and not having enough time. Was that you? Could you see the income or even profit your employer was earning? Could you see other business owners spending time with their family on holidays and at functions? Did you want to help others with your passion? Did you want to be in control of your own destiny? Work less, make more money, have more time, help others?

What was it?

When was the moment you said, "That's it! I am going to do this for myself!" Where were you? Who was with you? And who did you tell?

However the decision came about, I am sure we all had a similar vision. As my story goes I could see my business very clearly with my name up in lights. It was nothing short of perfection. I was the best, my business was the best and everything was wonderful. Right at that point of time when you made the decision to own your own business what did your future business look like? It may not look like that now but what did it look like right at that moment in your vision? How many staff did it have? How many days or hours were you working? How much money were you making? Every little detail.

While you have your vision clear in your mind, ask how your business compares with right now. Maybe not quite as perfect as your original vision. That's OK! It's not all about where you are right now. Yes, you have to know exactly where your business and life is right now but it's not the most important. You need to focus on how you are going to get your business and life to match the vision that you were dreaming of. If that seems a long way off, don't give up, it's probably closer than you think.

Every business is different and every business owner is different but that doesn't mean you cannot reach certain goals. You can be closer than you have ever been to your goals by following some really easy steps using your determination, focus and confidence. Yes, I said easy!

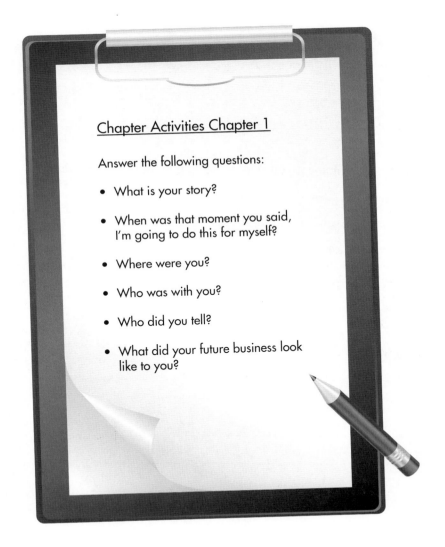

Chapter Activities Chapter 1

Answer the following questions:

- What is your story?

- When was that moment you said, I'm going to do this for myself?

- Where were you?

- Who was with you?

- Who did you tell?

- What did your future business look like to you?

Chapter Activities Chapter 1
Answer the following questions:

What is your story?

_____

_____

_____

_____

_____

When was that moment you said, I'm going to do this for myself?

_____

_____

_____

_____

_____

Where were you?

_____

_____

_____

_____

_____

Who was with you?

_____

_____

_____

_____

_____

Who did you tell?

_____

_____

_____

_____

What did your future business look like to you?

_____

_____

_____

_____

_____

_____

_____

> ## *It's not about what it is it's about but what it can become.*
>
> *Dr Seuss*

CHAPTER 2

Controlling your time

> *The best teachers are those who show you where to look, but don't tell you what to see.*
>
> *Alexandra K Trenfor*

CHAPTER 2

Controlling your time

> *He who controls your time controls your income.*

Let's talk about time. I know that by controlling your own time your business and life will be yours to control. You cannot continue to live in chaos at home or at work, this is a short lived scenario and cannot be sustained if you want to grow your business and make some serious income. While I am in control of my own time I am in control of my own income and the last thing I want is someone else determining how much I will earn this week, month or year. Many people say to me that they need to speak to their customers immediately or they will go elsewhere. I have tested and proven this theory in many businesses. When I owned my real estate offices, buyers would be very demanding of our time by arriving unannounced and would want to have a look at a property that instant. My receptionists' dialogue would always be, "Do you have an appointment?" They would answer "no" then she would say "oh!" and would raise her eyebrows in a motion to express that this was unusual. Then she would ask if they would like to make one?

Why did people expect real estate agents to be available in the office at any moment? The industry has not educated them! Sales people are so desperate for a sale they organise their day on the demands of others. At the end of the day they still haven't made a sale. Why not, you ask? Firstly nobody buys from a desperate salesperson and secondly an astute buyer does their homework, makes enquiries, plans and organises their day to inspect a number of comparable properties – sometimes with a number of agents, organises their finances in advance and gathers all of the relevant information prior to inspection, for example a copy of the contract and special conditions. Other industries have educated their clients well. You don't walk into your doctors' surgery to immediately see him/her without an appointment, nor your dentist, nor your surgeon, nor your bank manager, nor your solicitor, nor your accountant, nor you! Yes, that's right, if you educate your clients to make an appointment or let them know what times you are available each day or week for a phone call they will make sure they contact you in that given time, even eventually after they have called in a hundred times and haven't been able to get you until they call in during the advised appropriate time slot. Some clients do take longer than others to get used to not controlling your time. Now you may be reading this thinking yes, all good for some but not in my business, they will just go elsewhere. Will they? Is that a real fear or just your perception? I'm not saying for one minute that you must ignore your clients, because that is not good business. If your clients are aware that they can speak to you at an expected time and you do... then they will wait. Never make promises you cannot deliver. If you say you will contact them at a certain time, do it! How long they wait depends on the industry you are in but I know for sure, if I got to know your industry, the time you think they will wait and the time they actually will is very different. A lot of business owners I speak to say their clients accept 24 hours for a phone contact. Remember, we are not talking about making an appointment, this expectation is immediate even if the appointment is made for some time in the future. Other business owners say that their clients will accept same day return phone calls. Most business owners have this enormous fear of losing clients. In real estate, my team would only take a potential purchaser to look at a home after 48 hours from their initial enquiry. By doing this we could guarantee the owners at least 24 hours notice of any potential buyer inspecting their home. The team received many, many home owners' listings because this was a part of their service to their home owners. In other words, we earned a lot more commission by controlling our time. When we rang the buyer to confirm the appointment we could tell if they were just wasting our time as they would cancel with a trivial excuse as to why they were not going to buy. We could then assure the owner that we weren't wasting their time either. In my franchise business I would personally contact the potential franchisee only after four types of contact backward and forward between our office and the person enquiring. They received information, then they had to send information to us then they received some more information from us and so on. They were not discarded or not correctly looked after; they were given important information about their enquiry. This way we could 'shake the tree' and eliminate the people who would not proceed. Then we could spend more time only dealing with the genuine potential clients and not time wasters. Also, we could spend quality time with the potential franchisee not having to go through every detail but go through the questions they now had about the details. If a client contacts you and demands your time immediately, you have to ask yourself is this is the type of client you really want to have. Every time they want to speak to you they expect you to be available. I don't think so! In all of my businesses we have graded our clients and I will talk about this further on.

A default diary is an exceptional way to control your time. A default diary sets out your ideal week, notice I said ideal week not perfect week. This is not meant to be a perfect week, it's your ideal week. I have had people express huge resistance to a default diary using excuses like, "My industry is different," "It won't work with my customers" and "It won't work with my staff." You name it, I have heard it and these people soon lose credibility with me. For starters, they usually have not tried it and secondly have not bothered to ask me about what an ideal week is or why it's used. I use an ideal week to keep me focused on income producing work and not time wasting work. Some tasks can appear to be urgent but they are not important. I do the important tasks every day to grow my business fast and I have yet to find another method that works as well. Sure, it takes a little time to get used to it because you have to be self disciplined and tough on yourself at times but once you are in the swing of an ideal week you will never ever again be without one. I have had team members who never before in their career ever worked with an ideal week, but gave it a go and now they wonder how they ever coped in their demanding roles without one. Using a default diary and ideal week will dramatically change your working life, giving you more time, more life and of course more money. All of the successful people I know have a default diary and ideal week and so should you, you're successful aren't you? The ideal week is ever-changing and is not set in stone, which would be totally unreasonable. Every year I organise a national conference for my franchisees. I need to allocate more time to this conference at certain times of the year so I change my ideal week to accommodate this task for different months. That way I am in control and I know the time is being spent on something that is important in my business but doesn't always appear to be urgent.

It is easy to set up a default diary, what I need you to do is:

1. Take a few minutes to write down all of the things you do during your day. I often suggest that you keep your list with you over a week so as you come across a task you quickly write it on your list. If you try to just sit down and do it from memory you won't get very far and actually your list will be very short.

2. Allocate each job into a weekly diary giving the estimated time you think it takes to do each task.

3. Colour code each task with a different colour to easily distinguish the tasks across the week. The first ideal week you set up will change dramatically and quite quickly as you realise you may allocate too much time for one task and not enough time for another task. This is OK.

4. During your week, allocate what I call 'white time' (that's its colour too). This is for all of the jobs that hit your desk that are not regular weekly tasks.

5. Make sure you also have time in the ideal week for yourself as well; any business owner knows that usually their own personal time never makes it into their ideal week.

Some examples of tasks in your ideal week would be;

Emails – do not open an email every time it comes into your inbox. Set aside three or even four times a day when you check them, send quick replies or set another time aside in your white time to respond in more depth.

Team meeting – if you have staff, let them know what day and time you will meet with them and turn up, don't ever let them down. This way, they will not take up your time each day with smaller issues; they will bring those issues to the meeting and discuss them with you then. If it's just you making up the team, still allocate time to go over your goals and tasks for the coming week.

Accounts – paying the bills on time is important and shouldn't be done when someone rings you for money. If they do call, tell them that you do accounts on Monday at 10am (if that's your allotted time) and it will get paid then. Then make sure you do pay them at that time.

Social Media – if this is your responsibility, allocate the time but make sure you do not go over time because you got caught up in what someone famous was up to during the night. If you don't get it completed, allocate more time in your white time and finish it off then. Most importantly, stick to the ideal week.

If you allocate your time in your diary each day and don't give in to the pressures of other people's problems and demands you will have long-term successes. Be strong!

The way to be strong is to tell everyone around you that you are scheduling your time. Give them a copy of your schedule and ask for their help in achieving your goal. Tell your receptionist, your support staff or your wife/husband/partner. Ask them to be really nasty to you if you're not doing what you are supposed to be doing in the allotted time. Commit to a consequence if you don't. A friend of mine, Jamie, wanted to commit to an ideal week but just kept getting out of control so he asked his work colleague, Ben, for his help. Jamie gave Ben his ideal week. Ben had to check in regularly with Jamie to see what he was actually doing at certain times of the day. This was to check that Jamie was sticking to the schedule. If Jamie got side tracked and wasn't following the ideal day, Jamie was to buy Ben a bottle of wine. Ben held Jamie accountable every time. Ben may have been drunk doing it but it kept Jamie on track... I'm only joking about Ben not Jamie. Jamie very quickly got on track and never looked back; his income increased and so did his time at home with his wife.

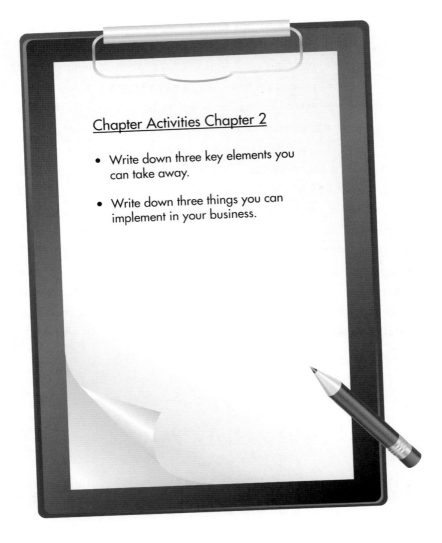

Chapter Activities Chapter 2

- Write down three key elements you can take away.

- Write down three things you can implement in your business.

Chapter Activities Chapter 2

Write down three key elements you can take away.

1 _____

_____

_____

_____

_____

2 _____

_____

_____

_____

_____

3 _____

_____

_____

_____

_____

Write down three things you can implement in your business.

ITEM	DATE TO IMPLEMENT BY
1	
2	
3	

NOW IMPLEMENT!

> # It's much more fun spending your time on the things that work.
>
> *Sharon Jurd*

CHAPTER 3

5 steps to freedom & success

"

SYSTEM stands for Save Yourself Time, Energy & Money.

Brad Sugars

"

CHAPTER 3

The 5 Steps to Freedom and Success

If you want financial freedom and a profitable business it's easy!

I believe there are 5 key areas of your business that if you focus on them regularly you create more time, more money and more life. If you want financial freedom and a profitable business it's easy! All you need to do is allocate a small amount of time to 5 simple areas of your business every day, week and month with consistency. The amount of time to allocate depends on where you are at in your business – are you just starting up or are you well established?

If you are a new start up business it is necessary to allocate time and to work on each of these 5 areas every day. If you neglect one of the areas you will find that your business will not be moving forward in the direction you want it to or more importantly at the speed you had wished for.

If you're an established business you must look at each of the areas and identify which areas you have neglected and which areas you have focused on. Then focus on the neglected area without sacrificing the other successful areas.

Whether you are a start-up business or well established you will need to spend more time on some area at different times of your business growth but the most important factor is to spend time on them all.

What business owners tend to do is work really hard on one area and they forget about the others. Then they realise that they need to work on a different area and again they focus all of their energy on that particular area. This type of strategy will not allow your business to grow fast! After all of the hard work you're putting in you will find minimal results. You will feel great for a while in the new area you are concentrating on but wonder why the other areas are failing.

The other thing that happens to business owners is that other distractions cause them not to work on all 5 areas. In this book we talk about controlling your time, you must be consistent with your strategy if you want results that seem otherwise unachievable.

As the saying goes, 'the grass is greener where you water it,' so spread your sprinkler around a little in every area and you will find the grass will grow greener than you expected.

The question is... are you ready to hear about the secret 5 Steps to Freedom and Success to ensure your business and financial success?

Are you ready to commit to these 5 easy steps? These areas are what I structure my businesses on and have had outstanding growth, quicker than predicted. In fact, every business I have started from scratch has reached a six figure income within the first 12 months of operation. If you want fast, rapid growth you must commit to this system. It's not hard work but its long term and some people have trouble with the long term bit.

5 Steps to Freedom & Success

These 5 areas are in no particular order as they are all as important as each other as my diagram shows you – there is no stop and start point, it's a flowing chart that never stops. I have only numbered them for ease of distinction in other documents like my ideal day/week, which I have spoken about in controlling your own time.

That list of 5 areas may seem pretty straight forward, or you might say obvious! The majority of people I speak with will admit being exceptional at a particular area but not really sure about others. Some say they have a great business and would love to strategically work on these areas to take their business to the next level but what a lot of people say is, Yes! OK! That's great! But what do I do now? So let's have a closer look at each one of these areas and discover what each area is actually about. What are some tools to get you started working on these areas and some great ideas on how to develop your existing efforts? If you are ready to grow your business fast that is!!!

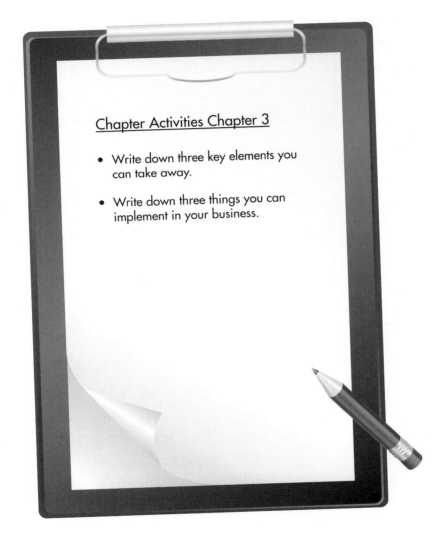

Chapter Activities Chapter 3

- Write down three key elements you can take away.

- Write down three things you can implement in your business.

Chapter Activities Chapter 3

Write down three key elements you can take away.

1 _____

_____

_____

_____

_____

2 _____

_____

_____

_____

3 _____

_____

_____

_____

Write down three things you can implement in your business.

ITEM	DATE TO IMPLEMENT BY
1	
2	
3	

NOW IMPLEMENT!

> *The people run the systems, the systems run the business.*
>
> *Sharon Jurd*

CHAPTER 4

Step 1: Database Management

> *It is no use saying we are doing our best – you have to succeed in doing what is necessary.*
>
> *Winston Churchill*

CHAPTER 4

Step 1: Database Management

5 Steps to Freedom & Success

If there is an area that I hear a lot of people having challenges with, it is database management. So why not start here. For most business people, especially the man in the van or owner operator, the last thing you want to do is come home after a long day and manage your database. It is really important to grow a database! Sometimes in business this is the only asset you have to really sell. Your chairs, computers and desks are worthless to say the least. Imagine if you could say to your potential purchaser I have a database of X amount of people, I have contacted them every month, I have all of their current details, I have their history of what business they have done with me and I have a system in place for repeat business with them which equates to $Y in potential income. Now wouldn't that be worth something to a potential buyer of your business?

> *Every business that I have owned has been set up to sell from the beginning.*

Every business that I have owned has been set up to sell from the beginning. Some business owners say to me, "But I'm not planning on selling any time soon." I know! But when you do, and you never know when that may be, you want to get the best possible price you can. A common reason for business owners to sell is their health and with bad health you don't get a lot of warning. Remember my story at the beginning of this book, I had no time to prepare and neither will you, so it's important to get it ready from the beginning. One day you will sell or close the doors and I would rather sell and get some return on my investment than close the doors and walk away with nothing. So what does setting a business up to sell mean? Have you heard of the stories of people owning and growing a business and out of the blue comes a buyer who offers them a lot of money; an amount the business owner cannot refuse? Why do you think that happens? Most of the time it is because the business has good systems and most of all a good database of qualified buyers. Every time I make a decision in my business one of the many questions I ask myself is, 'How will this decision help me sell my business?' Will it get me more clients to enter into my database? Will it give me more profit on the bottom line? Will it give the business more credibility? and, Will it help the business to operate without me? If the answers are yes then it's benefiting my business growth and its ability to sell.

Who do you enter into your database?

Here is your list broken into 5 categories. If you think of anyone else put them in as well!

Previous Clients – anyone you have done business with previously whether you think they may or may not do business with you again in the future.

Current Clients – anyone you are currently doing business with now whether you think they may or may not do business with you again in the future.

Potential Clients – anyone that has made an enquiry or someone you have given a quote to but has not done business with you yet.

Suppliers – anyone you do business with that supplies you with goods or services like your printing company, accountant, solicitor, broker.

Alliance Contacts – any businesses or people who may have similar clients to you or have clients that may require each other's services or who may offer a service to you in the future. These are very important as most businesses forget to database these contacts. These people can give you massive referral income now and in the future.

Friends & Family – These are the people who are your biggest advocates! You must make them feel bad if they don't hand out your business cards and refer you to their own friends and family. Use the guilt trip and any other method required. In all seriousness though sometimes family and friends don't think to refer you – let them know your expectations of them, give them plenty of business cards, tell them what you need them to do with the business cards. Again, sometimes they just don't realise what is needed from them to help you become a success. They will always want to help you and if you ask them they will gladly do what you ask. Remember to keep in contact with them to replenish the cards on a regular basis.

What information do you need to collect about the contact?

It is not just their name and address. I have made a list below of all of the details you require. If you don't have them, contact them and ask them. While you're there ask them for permission to contact them on a regular basis. All you have to say is, "Is it OK for me to send you some industry related information to you on a monthly basis via email?" you may have to collect this information over time with a few contacts but don't be lazy by just entering the name & address... you are better than that if you're reading this book.

Name – include partners name if relevant

Address – PO Box and Physical

Company Name

Landline phone number

Mobile phone number

Fax phone number – not used as often now but if they have one, get it

Email – there maybe more than one – this is the most important detail to get. If nothing else, get this information

Skype address

Trading times – only if this is relevant to your business

And to keep up with social media! More so for your personal contacts and alliances.

Facebook address

Twitter address

LinkedIn address

If you are just starting your business you are in the right spot at the right time because you have no mess to clean up and don't have a lot of clients (just yet). Start by adding all of those people I have just mentioned above into a Client Relationship Management software program. There are plenty on the market for little cost, it doesn't matter which one just get one that you feel will suit you, even in the short term – you can change as you grow. Use a spread sheet if you have to until you find one and then transfer them into the system.

If you are an established business and haven't added all of your previous clients etc. it is very important you spend an extensive time doing this. If you haven't got the time, hire someone to do it for you. They will probably be quicker and cheaper than you. You can be out selling while this is getting done. Use your invoice books, diaries or any other source you may have and get everyone and I mean everyone in there. Go through your business cards to collect details of all of your friends, family and alliances.

You will be very surprised at how many people you do know and have a relationship with. Now my disclaimer to this section is that we are not here to spam anyone or contact people you have not met so don't go through the yellow pages online please! If there is someone you are unsure whether to add just contact them and invite them for coffee or lunch or give them a call and simply let them know what you are doing and ask them using the dialogue I gave you above. We don't want people ringing and abusing you nor do we want you breaking any spamming or privacy laws.

What do you do with the database once you have entered everyone?

...when was the last time your data was cleansed?

A lot of business owners do have massive databases but do nothing about it. It is a waste of your time if you collect any form of data and don't act on it. When people say to me they have 3000 clients in their database I ask them, "When was the last time every single one of them were contacted?" and when was the last time your data was cleansed?" Cleansing your data just means the information is up to date and correct. People move house, change phone numbers, change jobs so you have to be sure you have their most up to date details. To cleanse data you send an email and see how many bounce back to you and then you contact them. You can do a mail out and see how many 'return to senders' you get. When clients do business with you ask them to update their information with you at time of booking the appointment. If you currently have an established database you can send them out a form asking them to update their information. Cleansing your data must be continual and regular. Customers forget to update their information with each and every company they have ever dealt with but when they need you again they will wonder where you have gone and will most likely go to your competitor.

When you know your data is cleansed you can begin to contact your database on a regular basis. How regular is up to you but don't be scared that you are contacting them too regularly. This question is regularly asked of me, "How often is too often?" Recently I heard it explained to me in an analogy of kisses! In presuming you like kisses, would you like someone to give you a thousand kisses? If they are good kisses and from someone you like, you ask? The answer would then be yes. Well, send your clients good kisses and they will love them a thousand times over. If you send them boring (sloppy) kisses they will unsubscribe! People like to be educated but they are sick of being told information. If you have something to educate your clients on they will read it. Now don't get upset if they don't read every single word in your newsletter every time, that's just your ego getting a little bruised. What happens most times is that the receiver will scan it and if there is nothing there that pops out at them they will delete the newsletter. That doesn't mean they will want to unsubscribe. If there is something there of interest they will read the article but what you should be surprised about is that a lot of the time they will see something that may interest someone they know and will forward it without themselves even reading it. And guess what? Now your newsletter is in front of someone not on your database and they may want to now subscribe.

You may want to target certain demographics in your database to offer certain specials, deals or offers at certain times of the year or reminders for them to do business with you again. You may want to inform them of something of importance that is affecting them. There are hundreds and thousands of reasons to stay in contact with your database so go ahead and send some kisses!

...go ahead and send some kisses!

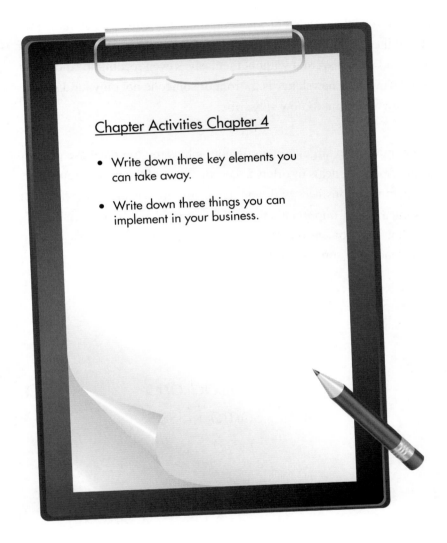

Chapter Activities Chapter 4

- Write down three key elements you can take away.

- Write down three things you can implement in your business.

Chapter Activities Chapter 4

Write down three key elements you can take away.

1 _____

_____

_____

_____

_____

2 _____

_____

_____

_____

_____

3 _____

_____

_____

_____

_____

Write down three things you can implement in your business.

ITEM	DATE TO IMPLEMENT BY
1	
2	
3	

NOW IMPLEMENT!

" Self discipline is the key to any success.

Sharon Jurd

CHAPTER 5

Step 2: Relationship Building

"

You are the end result of the people you meet and the books you read.

Charles Tarbey

"

CHAPTER 5

Step 2: Relationship Building

5 Steps to Freedom & Success

"

People buy from people!

"

I am always a big advocate of not just getting new clients but building relationships. People buy from people! It is much easier to do business with people you have a relationship with rather than trying to sell something to someone you don't know. Once you can get your head around this concept your business will grow fast! I quite often see people going to networking functions asking you what you do and then if in an instant they don't think they can do business with you they discard you like a piece of crap. The one thing they have achieved is that I remember their name and when I need to refer someone it will definitely not be to them. You may not do business with that person directly but they may have many clients and connections to help your business grow. You will not know whether they do or don't on your first meeting at a networking breakfast or lunch.

Just recently at a breakfast, I was standing with two gentlemen and one of the gentlemen asked me about my business, as I did with him. He was a business coach. I proceeded to tell him that I had a business coach in the same network and had done so for over 7 years. Immediately he assumed I was no longer a business prospect and quite abruptly ended our conversation by rudely (and I put that mildly) turning his back toward me and asking the other gentleman about his business in such a way that I was unable to participate in the conversation any further. I was left high and dry talking to my coffee cup. This gentleman has no idea that I have many thousands of people on my database with whom I have a relationship and which could equate to a lot of future business. All he was concerned about was the instant dollar he could have made from me. If you are focused on the immediate sale you will miss the many future sales to come.

> *...people who want to be educated are more likely to be open minded to learning about you...*

Now that I have had my little rant... back to the subject at hand, relationship building! I believe when you own a business you have to attend a lot of 'networking functions.' What types they are differs for everyone depending on their industry. Don't attend a women's networking event if you're not a woman! Choose events that have like minded business people, have possible potential clients, have business people that could become alliance partners and more importantly educate you – people who want to be educated are more likely to be open minded to learning about you and your business. Be aware that when you are at an event you are not there to tell them all about your business but to find out about them. Ask lots of questions not only about business but about themselves as this will give you a good idea on what they value as important, what areas they are focused on in their business and personal successes. If this person shows characteristics that you would like to build a working relationship with, organise to catch up outside the event for a coffee or lunch. By the way, this is not a dating event – just because they seem nice doesn't mean that they are worth building a business relationship with. Some 'nice' people are very bad business people and you may not want to associate yourself with that particular company or person. Use your intuition or your 'gut feel.' If you ask a lot of questions you will soon know enough about them to make a good decision.

Here is another rant coming... it's only one paragraph long so skip to the next paragraph if you're not interested. I met a lady who was a broker and who shall remain nameless. I offered her the opportunity to meet with 40 attendees at my upcoming franchise conference, all of whom had the possibility of doing business with her. She declined as she was too busy but the very next month during a conversation she was saying business was a bit slow so she had been attending some extra networking events to meet new people and continued to tell me about a function that she felt I should attend. The question I should have asked her was why she wasn't building a relationship with the people she already knew! My franchisees looked to me for direction and would have more than likely done business with her on my recommendation. This business income would have been a lot easier than slogging it out at every networking event.

If you are attending several different events you must be consistent, you can't expect to go along once then complain you didn't get any work from there and not go back. Would you like a little tip? If your answer is no, close your eyes now! You cannot expect to do business with someone if you haven't been in contact with them between 7 and 9 times. If you have met them once you cannot possibly expect to do business with them. If you want to do business with a person, ask yourself how many times you have contacted them. If it's less than 7 times you need to try harder! I'm not saying ring them 7 times in one day - you will be charged with stalking! But over a sensible period of time, ask them when they would like to be contacted again so you don't come across as pushy. If they want to deal with you then they will in their own time. Sure, there are dialogues and techniques that help with this process but that is all in my other book (that I'm now about to write).

When you attend a function, ask the attendees what other functions they attend and what type of demographic it attracts. Get a general feel about the event before attending. Relationship building takes time that's why you need to continually work at building lasting business relationships.

> *If you help someone to be successful you will be too.*

Build your alliances, they will refer you and you can refer them. For example, when a client of yours asks you for a good financial planner they are asking you because they know you, they like you and therefore trust that you will point them in the right direction. You need to be able, in an instant, to refer them to an alliance of yours and be 100% sure that the alliance you are referring them to will give them exceptional customer service. If an alliance looks after the person you referred to them with exceptional customer service they look upon this experience and give credit to you. If the alliance gives poor customer service that person will definitely blame you and they will also definitely let you know about the bad experience. Have the alliance's contact details in your phone so you can give them a call right away and let them know you have referred their business and for them to expect a call. Keep in contact with these alliances and make sure you really get to know them personally and really have a genuine care for their success in their business. If you help someone to be successful you will be too.

So in your business schedule, don't go out every day focusing on meeting new people all of the time, spend time building a foundation of relationships that will ensure your business will grow fast! If you can have multiples of people out there telling their friends and family how wonderful you are it will save you a lot of time trying to tell them yourself and they won't believe you anyway.

If they feel successful they will move heaven and earth to make you a success as well.

The other relationship I wanted to talk about here is the one with your staff. Sometimes business owners forget to build a solid relationship with their team. The bigger your team the harder it gets. You may be nice and pay well but I'm talking about really getting to know them. Take them out for coffee or lunch or even sit in the lunch room with them. I set a regular action (or task) in my diary called 'staff time.' When this action appears I focus on a particular team member I haven't spent time with of late. This is definitely not a formal meeting about work performance so don't make it so. Find out what their concerns are. What do they get excited about? What are their goals and aspirations? How can you help them get there? If you can get answers to these types of questions it makes it easier for you to help them succeed. It's not always about your success you know. If they feel successful they will move heaven and earth to make you a success as well. It's something that all business owners wish for – everyone in their team working to make the business a success! Imagine that! If you have a genuine concern for their success they will have a genuine concern for your success and that of your business.

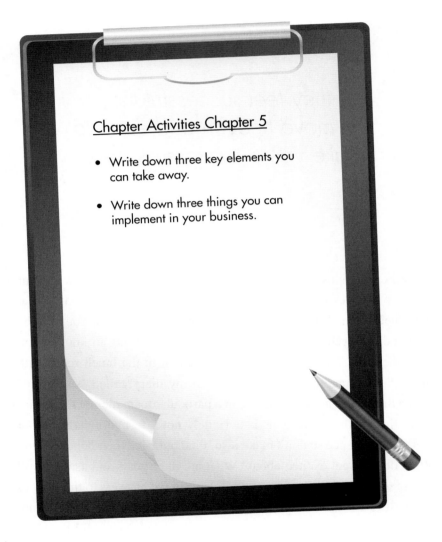

Chapter Activities Chapter 5

- Write down three key elements you can take away.

- Write down three things you can implement in your business.

Chapter Activities Chapter 5

Write down three key elements you can take away.

1 _____

_____

_____

_____

_____

2 _____

_____

_____

_____

_____

3 _____

_____

_____

_____

_____

Write down three things you can implement in your business.

ITEM	DATE TO IMPLEMENT BY
1	
2	
3	

NOW IMPLEMENT!

> *You can't grow your business alone. Everyone needs someone.*
>
> *Sharon Jurd*

CHAPTER 6

Step 3: Current Clients

> # If it is to be, it's up to me.
>
> *William H Johnsen*

CHAPTER 6

Step 3: Current Clients

5 Steps to Freedom & Success

So many people spend hours and hours on end trying to find new clients and forget about looking after their current clients. These are people who know you, like you and trust you. It is so much easier to do further business with these people, sell them other products and services you have. What I think is most important is that it is easier to get them to refer others to you.

To get them to refer other people to you, you have to be strategic about the timing of asking them to do this. You obviously can't ask them if they are no longer using your company or another supplier. You can't ask them well after you have delivered the product or service because they sometimes just forget to tell their friends and family and the WOW factor has lessened. Now let's not forget here that if you keep in contact with your current clients on a regular basis you will always be at the top of their minds. Here I'm talking about getting a testimonial or a direct immediate referral to someone they know that already requires your products or services from a very 'new' current client. People are most likely to refer you when they have just signed on the dotted line or they have just purchased the product or you have just completed the service.

In the subconscious mind, if they have just signed a contract with you they think you are the greatest professional in your industry. You have to be, they just chose you and they don't choose the most unprofessional person in the industry to do their work now do they? They won't have it said that they made a mistake and chose someone that is bad! Now their opinions may change if you do supply an inferior product or service but right at that moment they love you so you need to get them to tell everyone that you are the greatest, because they have just chosen you. They will if you ask them to, but you must ask them – set your expectation of them. They have set the expectation on what you need to do for them by way of supplying a product or service, now you have to set your expectation. Don't be afraid of this. You have to show some people who are not used to referring what they need to do. You can easily say, "I'm sure it's not too much to ask that at the BBQ you are attending this weekend you give my card out to at least four of your friends there and tell them how great I am, would that be

OK?" or "Please would you 'like' our Facebook page and write a short lovely comment on there for me?" Always ask them if that's OK; don't presume that they just will. Referring others can be very foreign to some people, especially if they are not in business and don't understand the importance of this to you.

It is extremely important to stay in contact with the clients who have done business with you. You need to be topmost in their minds so they will refer you to other prospective clients to potentially to do work with you.

I recently moved to the Gold Coast and I purchased a home. I needed my carpets cleaned and termite treatment prior to moving in but I didn't know anyone in the area. An acquaintance referred me to a friend of hers that did both. I contacted them, the process was simple and I had a wonderful experience, I never saw a spider for 12 months. But this is where it went downhill. I never heard from that company for the entire 12 months. I knew that I had to have the treatment done again but I could not remember the name of the company. I looked for the previous invoice but it had been archived. I never received a reminder or any contact at all. I couldn't even remember how much I paid so they could have charged me anything to make this 'to do' job get done for me. I would have been happy to have them come back and do the treatment and carpets again no questions asked... easy money for them I say! I had lost contact with the acquaintance as well so I looked on Google but no company name rang a bell. I had to then go searching my own contacts and alliances to see if they could refer me to someone new although I didn't really want someone new... they may not do as good a job. I did end up getting someone new and they didn't do as good a job but it was done. Did this original company shut their business, are they still operating, or did they go broke?? I don't know but what I do know is that if they did go broke I know exactly why. They didn't look after me, their current client who would have:

1. Paid anything (well almost but you get what I mean) to get the job done and;

2. Got the company back year after year with them simply prompting me to do so.

People work so hard at finding new clients that they forget or don't make time for the people already doing business with them.

People work so hard at finding new clients that they forget or don't make time for the people already doing business with them. Just one more thing before I finish this story; when I was contacting my own contacts and alliances to get a referral I had many say to me, "When you do find one let me know so I can do business with them too."

Your current clients like to hear about your successes and new innovations. They want to be involved with a company that is growing, moving forward and keeping up with technology within the industry. Again they want to be seen to be associated with these types of businesses. They brag to their friends, family and other business contacts but most of the time they don't know what you are doing. I have used an analogy, 'Peeing in your wetsuit' you are all warm and fuzzy but no one else knows about it! What benefit is it to the growth of your business if you have just pee'd in your wetsuit? By letting your clients know, it serves a number of purposes. Firstly, as I have said, they like to do business with successful businesses and secondly it is another excuse for you to get your name and brand in front of them to keep you at the top of their mind. If it is a new innovation, new product or a diversification in your business this will give them an opportunity to make further purchases with you.

When you offer a new product or service, different from what you already offer, you should immediately offer it to your current clients. They have already had a great experience with you so they are more likely to do further business with you. If you have given them a great experience and they haven't received a great experience from your competitor they will move their business to you straight away and with very little price resistance – even if you are more expensive than their current provider. By offering this product or service to them prior to the general public and promote it as such they will love the fact that you have thought of them and feel a sense of importance as a valued client to you.

With the advancement of technology we now have the luxury of being face to face with people who are remote to your location. This is a very powerful tool and should not be underestimated. Whether you use Go To Meeting, Skype or Facetime, just to name a few, the medium really doesn't matter. It's what suits you and your client at the time. It has often been said, "You can only do your best selling eyeball to eyeball." This point would be argued by many but I'm a true believer! You are able to use many more senses when you are looking right at the client. You can see if they are giving you their undivided attention, something you don't know on the telephone. You can assess their body language, their eye contact and body gestures. This greatly enhances your information gathering on whether they are happy with your product or service or not. If you decide to contact your current clients on a regular basis through a face to face medium they will, at first, be a little apprehensive, why? Because who else does that? After they get used to your contact they very quickly realise you have something important to offer them, update them on something, or genuinely have a real concern on how the product is going for them. I can sense you are questioning the time it takes to do this for every client. Yes, it does take time to make money and grow your business! I'm not saying that you have to contact every individual client you have especially if you have thousands of people on your database. What I am saying is, if you spend time with even a small number of clients who you believe will do more business with you then you won't have to spend double or triple the time and money trying to find new clients who may not spend one cent with you.

Just add up for me, using the figures in your business, if you spent 10 minutes of your time speaking with a current client and they upgraded their product or service, purchased another product or service from you and gave you a referral to a person who will spend the equivalent amount of money with you, how much would that be? Now add up the cost of a four week campaign in the newspaper for an advert (and the time to write and design the advert) and a networking membership (and the time attending every week) and a flyer drop of your community (and again the time writing and designing and delivery arrangements) to try and get the same result.

Which of the two figures makes more sense? I will bet the 10 minutes of your time with the cost of the internet connection for 10 minutes wins out in every scenario. And you don't even have to leave the office!! Am I exaggerating? NO! Try it in any situation, using any hard copy marketing, anytime, anywhere. You will not get better results than talking to the people who already love you!

To help you work out which clients to contact more often than others you must grade your clients. Whether it's A, B, C, or 1, 2, 3 or Platinum, Gold, Silver it doesn't matter. For this purpose I will use A, B, C. What matters is that you grade them. You then work with your A clients to continue to spend more often with you and continue to refer more people to you. Your A clients are known as your advocates or raving fans. They tell everyone about how great you are, they buy your product or service regularly – sometimes when they don't even need it. You decide on how you want to describe these clients and rank them accordingly. The A clients have to be looked after during the long term and not taken for granted. If you don't look after them, one day you will wake up and realise they now have a relationship with your competitor. They need to feel the love! They need to feel appreciated! Notice I said 'feel.' It is their perception of their importance to your business and this can vary from client to client. Ask them what they want from you and listen to them; then give them more. Don't give them something they don't want and never give them something you presume they do want – always ask! This is where face to face conversations are priceless.

You then need to work on your B and C clients and move them on up the ladder. You can offer incentives or memberships. You can offer them your discounts or promotional items or you can offer them something of real value - your time. You can even send a quick email to ask them how they are going with the new product or how they are enjoying the service. At first they will wonder what the hell is going on because I ask again... who does that? But if you do, they will remember you and tell everyone they know about you. And guess what? That now makes them a... yes that's right, a raving fan! And what do raving fans do? They continue to spend more money with you and refer you to more people. So you have moved them from a B or C client to an A client by contacting them. In your ideal day, allocate some time to B and C clients and soon you will be overwhelmed with A clients.

I haven't actually mentioned D clients. You know the ones. The clients that you spend 80% of your time on. The same clients that only contribute to 20% of your income. If you're lucky! Yes, most businesses have them. You are not the only one, so don't feel bad! There is something you can do with them; in fact, there are two things. Firstly, spend some time finding out what their issues are and change them to an A client. Easy! If that doesn't work, give them your competitor's business card and do not service them any longer. You can be nice about it if you want. All you have to say is, "I understand that we are not meeting your needs and I feel that your needs would be better met by another company. I would suggest you give ABC Pty Ltd a call and their contact number is xxxxxxx." Now that's a lot easier don't you think??? I know it is hard to tell clients you no longer want their money especially when things are really tough with profitability but more importantly, cash flow. Once you get rid of a few D clients you will be amazed at how much time you have to talk to your A clients. Do the maths again on how much you could earn by spending 10 minutes with an A type of client. It will be far greater than what the D client was spending. Fewer D's and more A's is how you grow your business fast!

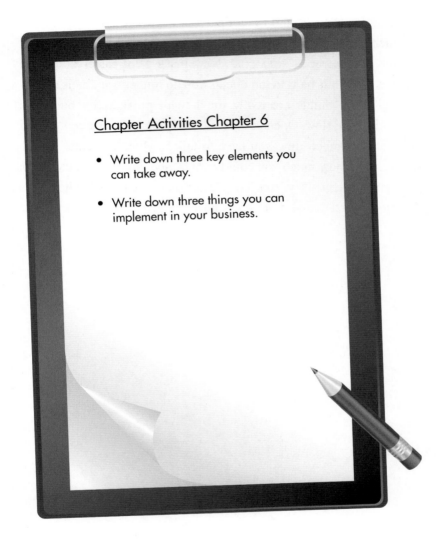

Chapter Activities Chapter 6

- Write down three key elements you can take away.

- Write down three things you can implement in your business.

Chapter Activities Chapter 6

Write down three key elements you can take away.

1 _____

_____

_____

_____

_____

2 _____

_____

_____

_____

_____

3 _____

_____

_____

_____

_____

Write down three things you can implement in your business.

ITEM	DATE TO IMPLEMENT BY
1	
2	
3	

NOW IMPLEMENT!

> *Everyday just do the single acts.*
>
> *Sharon Jurd*

CHAPTER 7

Step 4: New Clients

> *I think big. If you are going to be thinking anything, you might as well think big.*
>
> *Donald Trump.*

CHAPTER 7

Step 4: New Clients

5 Steps to Freedom & Success

As I said in the beginning of the last chapter most businesses actually spend most of their time in this area and forget about looking after their current clients. Wouldn't it be nice not to need any new clients? If you are a new business or an established business that has never looked after your current clients very well in the past (but not now after reading this book) you will need to spend some extra time here until you have enough repeat clients in your business. New clients come from varied sources and it is really important to document where each new enquiry comes from. No one should be put in your database unless they have an enquiry source. Some examples of an enquiry source are:

- Referral

- Website

- TV advert

- Yellow pages

- A particular mail out

- Networking event

- Group or organisation

Some examples of what an enquiry source is NOT:

- Call in

- Buyer

- Walk in

- Phone in

- Don't know

- Heard about us

- Other

Are you getting the general idea, it needs to be specific so you can measure where your marketing dollars are working best for you. I will give you a scenario. Let's say that your enquiries were broken up as follows:

44% website

23% came from referral,

17% came from networking events,

9% came from TV,

4% yellow pages,

2% mail out,

1% group/organisation

Knowing these figures, where would you allocate more of your budget/ time to next year?

a) Website as its working well?

b) Group/organisation because it needs improving?

Now there could be a lot of variables to this business and its scenarios but for ease of this demonstration most logically you would spend the majority of your time/budget on the website then referral and networking events. You could increase your TV coverage but it would be very costly and possibly difficult to increase the percentage but to increase your networking events may be more cost effective in obtaining a greater result. The purpose of this exercise was not to have a debate on what's right or wrong regarding marketing budgets. The purpose was to show you that once you know the figures you can make some informed business decisions that suit you, your business and your budget. If you want to increase your TV adverts go right ahead with confidence; you know your decision is informed and you're not just firing bullets at any source hoping for the best. In the next period compare figures and see if there has been an increased enquiry based on your efforts.

New clients must have an exceptional experience from day one but also on day 229 and day 587 and day 1574, if you get what I mean. How many of you know of a business where the first time you dealt with them they were fantastic, second time ok but by the third or fourth time they where awful! This is a very common mistake. The business owner is busy looking after the next new client. So set the standard for customer experience and make sure that every other time that client deals with your business it's exactly the same as day one. The question you are probably wanting to ask me is, that's all good but how do I get them in the first place? Good question! The most effective way to do this is to set up at least 10 lead generators into your business and then... those famous words 'test and measure.'

> *New clients must have an exceptional experience from day one but also on day 229 and day 587 and day 1574*

Let's firstly talk about lead generators. There are hundreds of lead generators but you need to have at least 10 going at any one time and no, this does not mean it has to be expensive. Depending on your business and your client demographic some will work better than others. Have a look at the previous enquiry sources – they are lead generators. Some other examples of lead generators are: Free media releases or editorials, car signage, fridge magnets, industry newsletter, cold calling, fundraising campaigns, expos, fetes, shows, strategic alliance, in store displays, window displays and school newsletters. Just choose what avenues you think will work and do those for a while it doesn't matter if it doesn't work the first time; you cannot expect to put one brochure in 5000 mailboxes and get 2500 enquiries. With some generators you have to be continual and consistent with your message and over time it will generate a large income enquiry but the message here is to choose 10 and start using them. This is called test! Then the next thing is to measure. For example, you have dropped mail in 5000 mailboxes and you don't know how many enquiries come in. You need to put a system or a dialogue in place to ask your new client, "How did you find out about us?" they will simply answer, "I saw your car in my street and got your number from there." Be very careful not to ask them, "Where did you get my number from?" because this may give you an incorrect indication as they may answer, "Yellow pages" but they may have seen your TV advert and then gone to the yellow pages to find your number. If you get incorrect information you may spend your advertising dollars on the yellow pages instead of a TV advert campaign.

> *Video testimonials are a very powerful medium to attract new clients.*

The best way, I believe, to communicate with new or potentially new clients is through video. It is a growing phenomenon. When people go to websites they now don't expect to just read everything they want to hear about it as well. They want to hear not only from you the company but from your current clients. Video testimonials are a very powerful medium to attract new clients. Let me say it again. Video testimonials are a very powerful tool to attract new clients. If you want to grow fast get ahead of your competition by having videos on your website, on Youtube, in your presentations, everywhere in fact – just everywhere you can think of. Other businesses are just catching on but it seems all too hard for them. They think they don't have a professional video camera, they don't have experience in editing and the list of negativities goes on. I'm going to go out on a limb here and say everyone has a video recording device with them most of the time. Correct me if I am wrong but whether you have a phone, smart phone, tablet, iPod, you name it, most devices have a camera and video. If you haven't, go get one! Put this book down and run out and get one now! If you have one, simply choose video in your camera section and press start, film, then press stop. Why people think it is too hard is that they think it has to be prefect with lighting, wardrobe, background etc. etc. This is nonsense! Your potential clients do not want to see perfection they want true, believable testimonials. If there is background noise, so what? It doesn't matter as long as you can hear what they are saying. Your current clients are not expected to be perfect so why would you portray them like they are? This will only alienate your new enquiry; they will not be able to relate to the 'fake' person in the video. If the video is of you as the owner – they don't expect you to be perfect either. My belief is that there are only two reasons why a person will buy from you. Are you ready for this? Get your highlighter ready. Care and knowledge! In that order and yes, only two! You can have the best product the flashiest flyers and adverts but if they don't think you care they will not become your client. Of course, they will also make sure you know about your industry and/or product. We will discuss how to become the industry expert in the next chapter. What better way to show the client that you care than using a video. They can see your body language, hear your enthusiasm and can make eye contact with you. They will love that you are not picture perfect but passionate about what you are doing and have a genuine care about them.

Have you ever heard the saying, 'People buy off People'? Well, you have now. I will explain. I previously went to a hairdressing salon and I still do so regularly in my ideal week. Remember that I suggested in the ideal week to make time for yourself? Well, that's my thing. I have shocking hair. Please don't turn and look at the photo because it's perfect??? The owner of the salon was my hairdresser and looked after me every week. I liked it that way. Then the owner announced that she was no longer working on Fridays, the day of the week that I went to the salon. She explained that she wanted to change days to have more time with her daughter; great what about me??? It's lovely that she is a mum first, sure, but don't get me wrong it's not about what her reason was, it could have been anything, but that didn't suit me. I now had choices. I could change my day. No, because I wanted my hair to look nice for the weekend. I could find a new hairdresser. OK, this might work but I was hesitant so, the very next week I get the new one... Oh no! She wasn't as good, why? Because she didn't get me a coffee straight away and didn't chit chat to me the whole time I was there about my favourite subject - growing businesses. She styled my hair nicely, but she wasn't the same. So are you getting the point now? I didn't love the business, I loved the person. Why did I tell you this story? From this book you have learnt that you must give your client the same experience every time from day one, or day 1597 even if it is with another team member and have the systems in place so that your team knows what is expected of them; like getting me a coffee straight away!

You must change your business from a strange company logo to a caring, knowledgeable person. How you can do this is by video message. By watching a video they get to know you, your body language, mannerisms, smile etc. and then they will say, "I like this person so therefore I trust this person and will do business with them." If you appear to be a real, caring, human being – not perfect, they will want to do business with you.

So what was the happy ending to my above story, if you care to know? I changed hairdressers and found a lady that was knowledgeable, caring and made great coffee! You had to have known I was going to say that?

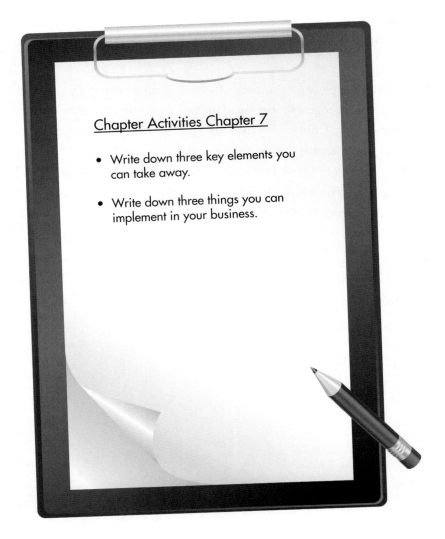

Chapter Activities Chapter 7

- Write down three key elements you can take away.

- Write down three things you can implement in your business.

Chapter Activities Chapter 7

Write down three key elements you can take away.

1 _____

_____

_____

_____

_____

2 _____

_____

_____

_____

_____

3 _____

_____

_____

_____

_____

Write down three things you can implement in your business.

ITEM	DATE TO IMPLEMENT BY
1	
2	
3	

NOW IMPLEMENT!

Each day brings you much closer to your goal.

Sharon Jurd

CHAPTER 8

Step 5: Self Promotion

Definition of Character: to carry out a resolution long after the mood in which it was made has long left you.

Charles Tarbey

CHAPTER 8

Step 5: Self Promotion

5 Steps to Freedom & Success

I want to say straight up – don't get all shy or embarrassed about promoting yourself. You don't have to be the life of the party to get everyone to know who you are and depending on what type of party it is, this may not position you as the expert in your industry. I must admit that it took me the longest to recognise its importance in this area of my business for my fast business growth. For a very long time I was very successful in what I was doing and achieving but I wasn't known as the expert. I wondered why other people in my industry were asked to comment in the paper or on the radio, television, etc. but in my opinion they were far from being the expert in their industry. Why hadn't I been asked to comment? I would ask myself and then I would start making all sorts of excuses, blaming people and generally having a good old bitch session about my competitor instead of doing something about it. I would just go about growing my business faster and being more profitable thinking that the media and the like would eventually notice me and my achievements. Well, that didn't happen. My mentors would say things like, "You are the best salesperson I know" or "You give the greatest customer service in any business I know" and "You grow businesses like no other" but still the people outside my business didn't see this at all.

> *For a very long time I was very successful in what I was doing and achieving but I wasn't known as the expert.*

At this point you would be thinking I had some lightning bolt moment about self promotion and the benefits to my business. Well, it's sad to say I did not. It came down to my ego...I wanted my name up in lights, my face on television, my voice on radio. Yes, it is a bit embarrassing to say it was all about my ego but I couldn't stand being second best to my competitor. I am being truthful here so I hope you appreciate my honesty but really it doesn't matter what my driving force was to begin with, along the way I realised that my ego had to get out of the way and I learnt that by self promotion I was benefiting my business and life. So, my point is this; it is not about ego but about growing your business by being positioned as the expert. Some people say they don't like the term expert. I say, get used to it if you want success. If you say it over and over again to yourself you will believe it. In the beginning, if you really feel uncomfortable, use other words like specialist or No.1 or sought after, but don't just stay in your comfort zone; try it and soon you will see how easy it is. Try now! Just say to yourself I am the ... expert. Here are some examples; I am Australia's No.1 electrical expert. I am the most sought after wellbeing life coach. I am the business growth specialist.

I want you to write yours down on a piece of paper, stick it to your mirror and say it to yourself several times every morning when you are doing your hair or cleaning your teeth. You will soon get used to it and you will soon believe it. Say it every time you meet someone new – they don't know you feel uncomfortable, they will just believe you.

Awards give you lots of credibility in your industry. Enter every event for an award known to man that you can. Some business owners say to me that certain awards aren't that important and the events are not run well, or they favour certain businesses and they have the same winners each year. I disagree. It may not sound that exciting to you but to the consumer or general public it gives huge credibility and a perception of success. I have entered events where it appeared the same winner won it every year. I won the first time I entered; it was because the same business had no competition year in and year out. Then I started to win every year! I set a new benchmark and then I had no new competition. That's just how it works. When you enter, if you have a good business, you will win.

When you do win, this usually gives you great opportunity to promote you success through different types of media. Most times the local media is free for the winner of the award. Then you can promote it through social media, website emails and any other form you choose to use. It gives you a reason to contact your current and prospective clients and let them know they are or will be associated with an award winning business. Even if you are only a finalist for the award you should still promote this through your business, sometimes just being a finalist is an excellent achievement in itself.

Firstly, search your local area and find out what awards are being given and make sure you enter. Look further afield into your industry nationally then outside your industry. Set the dates in your diary for the opening of submissions so you do not miss any.

I know what you're thinking; I don't have time to fill out all of these award submissions. I ask, why not? But that's a whole other chapter in this book called Controlling Your Time. Once you have filled out one award submission the others will be very similar and you just have to modify each. They will always ask for your photo and BIO so once you have done that you won't have to do another one, you just need to keep it updated. Usually they ask for a background on your business story. Again, once it's done just copy and paste and so on. They all appear to be different applications but they are usually very similar. If you really don't want to spend the time on this, hire someone who does. There are plenty of PR (Professional Relationship) firms that will do all of this for you. As you enter larger, more national or international award events you will see they are a must.

With awards you just never know when they will come in handy. I still mention awards I have achieved over 10 years ago because it is relevant to what I want to achieve today. Customers don't really care how long ago the award was achieved, just that you did achieve it. My awards have got me through doors that I could not otherwise get through.

Another area of self promotion that positions you as the expert is a blog. If you haven't written a blog before it is actually quite easy once you start. In one of my businesses, HydroKleen Australia, we basically clean dirty air conditioners. At first I wondered how many times I could tell my customers that they had a dirty air conditioner and that they needed to clean it and why anyone would read something as riveting as cleaning dirty air conditioners. Then someone asked me the following question, "What do you want to achieve from your blog?" My answer was, "I want to increase my credibility, I want to be seen as the expert, I want to help my Google search by updating my website regularly." I didn't actually mention that I wanted someone to clean their air conditioner! Oops! The next thing that this person asked me was, "Well, why are you worried about whether people are going to read it or not?" I had a feeling this was becoming a light bulb moment! I had to think about this for a moment and I want you to as well. If I was using it to increase my credibility and to position me as an expert why was I so worried about people reading it? It took me a moment to get it. I was so hung up on the fact that people may not like 'me' or be critical of what I write and forget why I was writing it. So I focused on not trying to be the greatest writer of all time but to just write something. Once I got my head around this I was on my way to blogging success! Well, in my opinion anyway. There are lots of people out there sharing their expertise in blogging and if you want to earn real dollars from blogging take up their systems and go for it. If it's just a self promotional tool for your business just follow a few simple rules or mine.

1. Don't rave on about irrelevant things – people will not read a whole novel in a blog. In this format we are using it to keep you foremost in your customers minds, give credibility and position.

2. Use other peoples links – that way you don't have to write a whole article just tell a bit of your story and then refer them to the article you recently read.

3. Write a blog often – depending on your industry the timing is up to you but more often is better than not enough. So, if your first thought is monthly then do it fortnightly just to be safe.

4. Tell everyone you meet that you have a blog – don't worry if they don't follow your blog; if you worry that's your ego getting in the way. They may just generally not be interested in what you have to say in your blog. That doesn't mean they won't do business with you. You are just building credibility with them; don't forget what you are using the blog for.

5. Talk to them directly – use dialogue so that they feel you are talking to them alone and not to a mass of people. They will feel connected to you and will quickly form a relationship with you.

I must mention that even though we are very clear on what we are using the blog for in this instance, hopefully your content will help a customer or their alliance with some useful and informative information and teaching. If you get really good at writing content, potential customers will do business with you. Your content must be aimed at helping anyone with some useful information. Do not sell to them or promote your product, this is not the forum for direct selling.

My secret tip is to sit down and write a number of blogs and save them so you are not rushed to put something together on the day the blog is due to go out. So get to it and start writing, you will be surprised at how easy it becomes.

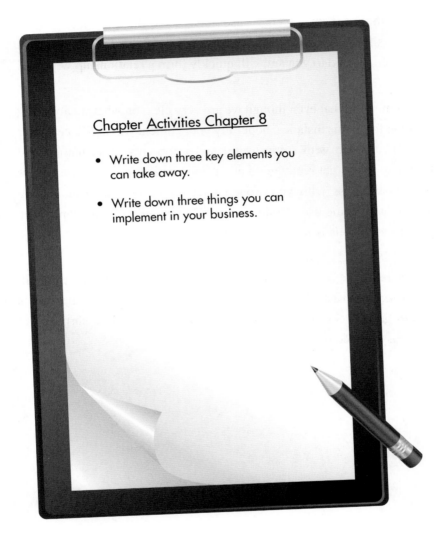

Chapter Activities Chapter 8

- Write down three key elements you can take away.

- Write down three things you can implement in your business.

Chapter Activities Chapter 8

Write down three key elements you can take away.

1 _____

_____

_____

_____

_____

2 _____

_____

_____

_____

_____

3 _____

_____

_____

_____

_____

Write down three things you can implement in your business.

ITEM	DATE TO IMPLEMENT BY
1	
2	
3	

NOW IMPLEMENT!

66

Start somewhere you never know where you will end up, it maybe where you want to be.

Sharon Jurd

99

CHAPTER 9

A Worry or a Concern?

What if it doesn't work? Ask yourself what if it does?

Pat Mesiti

CHAPTER 9

A Worry or a Concern?

I want to talk to you about the difference between a worry and a concern as I feel it is really important to differentiate between them when growing your business fast. I'm going to use a simple analogy to explain it to you. I feel that a lot of business owners won't allow their business to grow fast because of worries and concerns. I have had one lady explain to me that once she understood what a worry was and what a concern was she could then allow her business to flourish and she did not hold back any longer. So bear with me while I explain.

> *You shouldn't worry*
> *about a worry!*

You shouldn't worry about a worry! A worry is when you are giving thought to something that hasn't happened and you think might happen in the future. You project in your mind what might happen. You play the situation out and figure what you will say and do when this situation may occur. You spend time thinking about it, talking to others and getting their opinions on the yet to happen event. Sometimes this proposed event may have nothing to do with you; it may be a friend or family member's situation that is consuming your thoughts and time. A concern is when the event is happening or happened and you need to deal with a real life event. Here is an example: You have Christmas coming up and all of the family are planning a large get together and your two brothers-in-law have had a verbal argument during the year that hasn't been resolved. You start to get worried! You don't want them to spoil the day, you don't want them upsetting anyone and you don't want the children to experience this type of confrontation. You speak with your sisters and other family members discussing what you will do and what they will do if they start to argue. Now this is clearly a worry. You are contemplating something that may or may not happen. You may get to the Christmas gathering and see that the two brothers-in-law are laughing and having a great time. You realise you have spent lots of time worrying about something that never eventuated. Now let's explore the scenario that they had a verbal argument at the Christmas gathering. This clearly becomes a concern. Once you have identified a concern you ask yourself if this is your concern or someone else's concern. The two men arguing are the ones that have the concern. If they argue and cannot settle their dispute, should it be a concern for you? If it was a direct argument with you it is your concern to deal with accordingly. So, each time you feel yourself worrying about something ask yourself these questions:

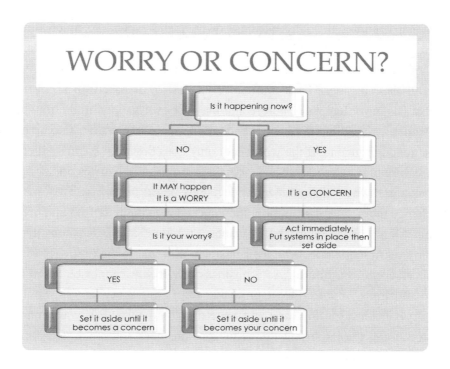

The question I get asked most often is if there is something that you do have to consider before it happens e.g. retirement, you cannot just forget about it until it happens. Sure, things like retirement and death have to be dealt with before they happen. What is needed is for you to put a system in place to deal with the issues, like superannuation payments, funeral plans and insurances. You get those in place to stop the worry and put them aside until you have to periodically review and reassess them, then you put the worry aside again. You don't have to continually worry about something that hasn't happened.

When it comes to many business owners, they spend so much time worrying about a worry they never make the decisions that will allow their business to grow fast! They subconsciously (or even consciously) hold their business back and can even destroy it based on an event that has never happened before and may not ever happen in the future. People worry about not having enough money if interest rates go up or not enough income if the world economy goes down. In business there are variables every day. These variables are usually worries and some business owners make business decisions based on worry. They may change their stock distribution, they may change their staffing and they may even change their whole business structure. These decisions may have detrimental effects on their business now and in the future (if they survive into the future). As a business owner you cannot be reactive to situations, you need to be proactive and I am not saying you should bury your head in the sand and hope things go away. But you cannot stop doing the important things in your business and make decisions based on a worry and lose focus on what is growing your business and bringing you great profit. My point here is to stick to a structured plan of business growth and don't get caught up in a distraction. When worries become concerns make sensible business decisions and act quickly. Usually people will act slowly when making decisions, don't! Act quickly and smartly and you will survive any concern that comes your way.

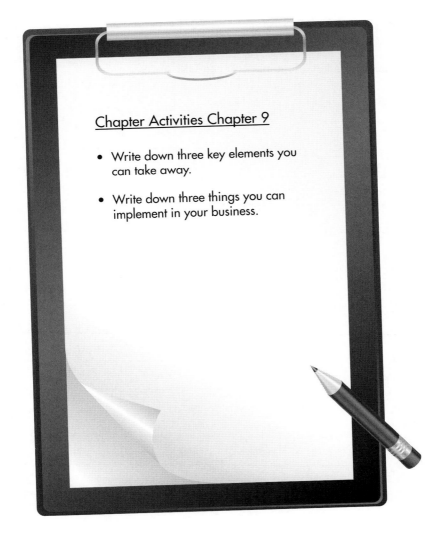

Chapter Activities Chapter 9

- Write down three key elements you can take away.

- Write down three things you can implement in your business.

Chapter Activities Chapter 9

Write down three key elements you can take away.

1 _____

_____

_____

_____

_____

2 _____

_____

_____

_____

_____

3 _____

_____

_____

_____

_____

Write down three things you can implement in your business.

ITEM	DATE TO IMPLEMENT BY
1	
2	
3	

> *It's what you think*
> *– not others.*
> Sharon Jurd

CHAPTER 10

Why don't some Businesses Grow Fast?

"

Do not confuse motion and progress. A rocking horse keeps moving but does not make any progress.

Alfred A Montapert

,,

CHAPTER 10

Why don't some Businesses Grow Fast?

In this book we talk about the simple steps to growing your business fast so I thought it was important to talk about why there are businesses out there that seem to be a great business with good ideas but never really ever 'make it' or even worse, close up. Or why is it that plumber A's business is growing by the day while plumber B's business seems to be struggling or even dying. For this purpose we will presume they are servicing the same clients, in the same area, charging a similar amount of money to their clients for the same service and they are both competent plumbers. There is really no difference on the surface between the businesses, so why are they so different in their success and speed with which they are growing?

Throughout my business life I have seen this scenario time and time again. This book is here to help yours be the business that is growing faster than that of your competitor but I have been asked before – if it works and it's easy, why not? Why isn't plumber B following these easy steps? There are a number of reasons and if you find that you have the same excuses I am going to talk about shortly you can change your thoughts and make a big difference to the speed of your business growth.

Firstly, I have found with the businesses like plumber B's, the owner has no real vision on where the business is heading. A vision cannot be just a dream you had one day and you do nothing about working towards it. In business it takes a plan to help you achieve your vision. The steps you need to take or things you have to do to get there. Then you work every day at doing the things that are taking you one step closer to your goals. What happens is that a lot of business owners like plumber B are very busy doing things but they are not getting any closer to where they want to be. A busy business may not be a growing business. Plumber A is focused on what has to be done and keeps moving forward, closer and closer to his vision.

How is plumber A getting to his vision? He has perseverance and he is very consistent in what he does. No-one ever achieves their dream overnight (argue if you will). It might seem that sometimes people do – like athletes, we don't see their perseverance and consistency, we just see the race that they win. Like my competitors, they watched my wins and never saw that those wins came from perseverance and consistency. Some people say, "They were in the right place at the right time" but that is totally false – in my opinion of course. That person was in the right place because they deserved to be there. They had perseverance and/or consistency that is now paying off. Being consistent is not hard it just takes some getting used to. What plumber B does is, he goes and secures new business then he gets busy doing the new jobs. Because he is so busy he no longer looks for new clients or no longer has the time to service his current clients correctly. Then the work runs out so he starts looking for new business again then the whole cycle starts all over again. Plumber B's work is up and down and so is his cash flow and profit. Plumber A would allocate time each week to ensure he consistently looked for new business and looked after his current clients. Plumber A's work is therefore consistent and so is his cash flow and profit.

I will give you an example of one of my franchisees. When he started his franchise he set a target to deliver a certain number of information packs to prospective clients each and every week for a set number of months. At first he was getting some work from the brochures but a small percentage compared with what was given out. He thought at times that it wasn't working and a waste of time, money and maybe it was different in his area, but he continued. 15 months after he had given the brochures out he was still receiving work from them. Calls were coming in every day and week. In his second year of operation he was the largest income earner and largest profit earner within the franchise. He was working less in the business and now working on it and over 3 years grew his business by a 100% increase each year and he continues to do so. What would have happened if he did not persevere with his consistent delivery of those brochures? That wasn't an option for him.

Getting back to our example of plumber A and plumber B, when they started their business they were both very competent plumbers. What changes in business over time is their personal growth and education. Plumber A attends seminars, training sessions, webinars and so on to further his knowledge not only in his industry but in business. Plumber B hasn't got time – he is too busy plumbing. Plumber A learns to grow his business, give greater customer service and discovers new advancements in the industry to help his business and clients. Plumber B is still doing things the way he has done them for the last 20 years. He was taught to do something when he was an apprentice and never explored the option of change. A fast growing business is forever changing. Growing businesses don't change for change sake; they continue to do what works. By putting testing and measuring in place for new implementations, growing businesses know what is working and they continue to refine and improve what they do to achieve their goals. Sometimes change can be considered a risk. In business you have to take risks. If your change is controlled, the risk will be minimised.

> *No one can grow a business alone!*

What plumber A has shown by attending seminars and training sessions is that he is not afraid to get help. No one can grow a business alone! Everyone needs someone to help them get there. Whether its staff, a franchisor, an accountant, a solicitor or a mentor. Every successful person has a coach; successful golfers, athletes, entrepreneurs, singers, dancers. You name the genre and they have a coach. So why do business owners feel they don't need one? A lot of the time owners are very good at what they do, like our plumbers A & B they are very competent at plumbing. Just because you are good at what you do does not guarantee a successful business. You must grow personally to grow your business. What plumber A did was let go of his ego, thinking he knew everything and opened his learning to take him and his business to a whole new level. Having a coach will keep you on track and give you motivation when you need it the most. Go on, admit it, some days we just aren't as committed or enthusiastic as we might like to be.

My next point is businesses following the crowd. If plumber A continued to do what plumber B is doing he would get the same result. If you want better results than your competitor don't do the same thing that they are doing. If you need to copy, find someone else who is not your competitor and who is achieving what you want to achieve, then copy them!

I have what seems like a trivial example but I find it very relevant. I saw a Facebook friend of mine post on her wall the question as to whether or not she should put a photo on her business cards. Now our marketing and PR friends would have very strong views on what is 'right' or 'wrong' but that's not the point here. This lady got a number of points of view from all types even down to comments such as, "Only sleazy real estate agents put their photos on their cards and who would trust them?" This really hit home for me considering real estate is a passion of mine and I am currently a registered real estate agent and don't consider myself sleazy. Anyway, I'm getting side-tracked; this is not about my opinion. After a large number of people told her not to put the photo on the cards she said, "I have deleted the photo." This suggested to me that she already had the photo to go on the card in proof form but because of less than a dozen comments from people who, based on their comments and a little investigation by me, didn't appear to be her clients or even own a successful business in her industry she made a business decision to conform to the majority or the crowd. She was afraid to stand out and ended up doing the same thing everyone else is doing. If you do the same thing every other mediocre business is doing you are also going to be mediocre. Why didn't she follow her own business instincts and then test and measure? Are you following the crowd? I have heard from businesses that are not so successful who say, "This won't work in this industry" or "This won't work in my area." Well, keep doing what you are doing then and stay out of the way of the business owners who are doing it in your area.

Looking at these excuses or reasons (whatever you would like to call them) for not growing your business fast, it seems that there is a common denominator in each of them. Did you pick it? There was no real vision, no perseverance or consistency, no structure or system, doing the same thing forever, scared to be different, following the crowd, afraid to get help. Well I will help you out, it was the business owner. Plumber A makes choices to learn, improve and grow, plumber B doesn't. Which plumber are you?

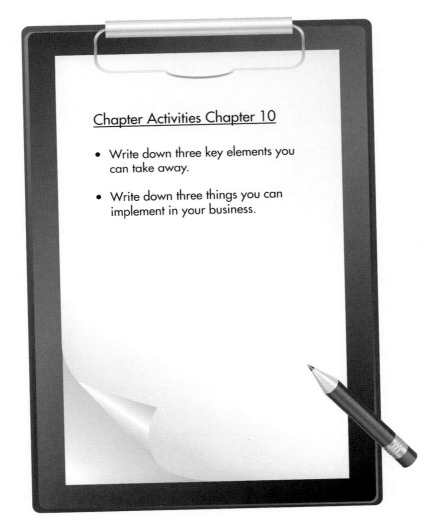

Chapter Activities Chapter 10

- Write down three key elements you can take away.

- Write down three things you can implement in your business.

Chapter Activities Chapter 10

Write down three key elements you can take away.

1 _____

_____

_____

_____

_____

2 _____

_____

_____

_____

_____

3 _____

_____

_____

_____

_____

Write down three things you can implement in your business.

ITEM	DATE TO IMPLEMENT BY
1	
2	
3	

Don't get sidetracked by people who are not on track.

Sharon Jurd

CHAPTER 11

How has your Business changed?

"

For your life to change...first you must change

Brad Sugars

"

CHAPTER 11

How has your Business changed?

Every day our businesses are changing. If you don't like change then owning your own business may not be right for you and I'm sure you wouldn't still be reading this book if you couldn't cope with change. So I will presume you have love change!

Are you a conference junkie or do you know of one? You know... the people who attend every conference and seminar that is scheduled. You go along yourself and sure enough, the same person or people are there too. This same person buys every pack of CD's and books for sale. Takes them home and uses them for a door stop. Yes, a door stop! They don't read the books and they don't listen to the tapes. OK, I will give them a bit of credit here, they might listen to a few of the CD's or they might read a book or two but what they don't do is implement what they have learnt. They know that what the trainer is saying works but they just don't make the changes in their business or their life to get results. Am I talking about you? I'm hoping not! These people then make excuses saying that it's too time consuming and that they have been really busy, they have started, you have heard it all before. Then the very next week they are attending the next conference to learn about something new to improve their business and buy another lot of books and CD's. Their businesses haven't grown or improved or had any significant change. Then they are usually still saying the same things like, 'times are tough,' 'been working long hours,' 'yeah, I have been busy and there are not enough hours in the day.'

I know that the majority of the books and CD's would have worked very well to improve their businesses; these educational tools are not a waste of money. They just didn't use them in the way they were intended. After the conference or seminar, if you do not go back and use what you have learnt in order to make changes in your business or life you will be the same as you were the day before and you will be the same tomorrow... attending another conference... why would you keep spending your hard earned dollars and not implement what you have learnt? People are looking for the quick fix to instant success but are never prepared to make change. If you see, hear or meet someone that is doing what you want to do, well then, copy them! Do what they are doing. But what happens is that some people aren't prepared to have perseverance and consistency, they want it now without changing their behaviour.

In each of the previous chapters we have covered a lot of ground. What I would like to do now is see how you went with implementing the relevant changes in your business and celebrate the successes you have had.

Why your own Business?

Did you identify why you wanted to start your own business?

Who was the first person you told?

Did you write how you would like your business to look?

What were the benefits of these?

Controlling your Time

Did you take control of your time?

Who was the person that kept you accountable?

Did you design an ideal day?

What were the benefits from these?

Database Management

Are all of your contacts entered?

Did you cleanse your data?

Did you send some kisses?

What were the benefits of these?

Relationship Building

Did you attend a networking function?

Have you spent time with your staff?

Did you meet up with someone after a networking event?

What were the benefits of these?

Current Clients

Did you grade your current clients?

Did you make contact with a current client?

Did you ask a new client for a referral?

What were the benefits of these?

New Clients

Did you start collecting enquiry sources?

Did you make a video?

Did you find 10 lead generators?

What were the benefits of these?

Self Promotion

Did you enter an event to win an award?

Did you start a blog?

What expert name did you give yourself?

Worry or Concern

Did you identify your worries?

Did you identify your concerns?

Did you stop worrying about worries?

What were the benefits of these?

> # When you do, you will get.
>
> *Sharon Jurd*

AUTHOR'S FINAL WORD

You must have desire and passion to succeed. Some people want to succeed but do very little about it but talk. This book was designed to make real change in your business. If you follow these easy steps they become the same habits that all profit driven business owners have. Business owners who have financial freedom through their businesses are not extraordinary people they are just consistent people. They know what they have to do on a daily or weekly basis in a controlled manner to get them to where they want to be.

You have the vision of what you want your business to look like, you now have the secrets to what fast growing business owners are doing. If you have implemented these proven steps in your business along the way, while reading this book, you will now be experiencing big effects from some small changes.

If you grow your business fast, this will give you more money, more time and more life. Create the lifestyle you want to achieve through your business. Don't be a slave to long hours, D grade clients, and no cash flow or profit. Follow these methods and you will be surprised at how quickly things can change. Keep implementing!

I wanted to finish off with a little story of my own. Just yesterday I was going to an important corporate event and as any good woman would know, it takes time to choose the outfit. I wanted to be professional but 'spring time' relaxed. This is a hard combination to pull off for someone like me. As you do, I tried on what seemed like a hundred different outfits or combinations of outfits. In my desperation and my exhaustion I came across a dress that was in my wardrobe that I hadn't worn for some time, I'm talking quite some time ago. We don't need to go into timeframes here but I must confess I was very proud of myself that I could actually still fit into the dress. It was just what I was after. Why hadn't I worn it lately? I couldn't remember why I hadn't worn it, but I did know I had worn it a lot. So I decided to wear it. When I attended the function I was surprised at how many positive comments I received about my outfit. I was shocked to say the least; it boosted my self esteem as well. So, sure enough I washed the dress and hung it in the wardrobe, front and centre for the next occasion. I thought about why I hadn't worn this dress recently. Why did it end up in the back of the wardrobe? Was it because new dresses had come along? Then I realised I had found the new flavour of the month in my new purchases. The new 'in' fashion statement was hanging in the front of my wardrobe and the proven dress was at the back. This is the same in business. Business owners are always looking for the next 'fashion statement' and forget about all the proven strategies they have had in place in their business. Have you said to yourself while reading this book, "I used to do that, but I don't do it now." If you have, ask yourself why you aren't doing it now. Growing your business fast is about doing the simple things in business, there is no complicated formula. So bring that proven strategy, which we have talked about in this book, to the front of your wardrobe.

"

*It is always
up to you.*

Sharon Jurd

"

ABOUT THE AUTHOR

Sharon Jurd

Entrepreneur, Author, Speaker, Business Mentor and Success Coach

Sharon is a highly respected International best-selling Author as well as a seasoned Business Executive, Entrepreneur, Growth Strategist and Success Coach.

She is passionate about helping people grow their business faster than the competition by giving those business owners financial freedom, and the choice to live the life they deserve.

Sharon is qualified and recognised as a leading business coach, licenced business agent, licenced real estate agent, licenced auctioneer, licenced stock and station agent and she holds a diploma in business and franchising.

Sharon's passion for peak performance and creating success started just 6 months after she opened her first real estate office as a Century 21 franchisee, she obtained a 72% market share despite having six major well established competitors. Within the year Sharon had opened her second office and quickly became a major player in that market place too – as the youngest single female director within the organization.

After dominating in this area Sharon went looking for a new challenge and sold her successful awarding winning real estate offices.

Sharon is the director of her own franchise network "HydroKleen Australia" and grew it massively in just 2 short years making it the leader in its field.

Her professional achievements have been recognized by her winning over 17 industry and business awards such as Franchise Business of the Year, People's Choice Award, Chamber of Commerce Business of the Year, Gold Coast Business Excellence Award - Emerging Business and Merit Award for Franchise Women of the Year NT/QLD just to name a few.

For more than 20 years Sharon has worked, travelled, consulted and taught internationally, speaking to and motivating thousands of people in Australia, New Zealand, England, France, Italy, United Arab Emirates, USA, and Canada on how to create wealth and financial success.

Sharon's achievement and motivational programs plus articles published in newspapers and magazines nationally and internationally, have made her a sought-after speaker and consultant on the international stage.

She is the international author of the book "How To Grow Your Business Faster Than Your Competitor – *The Secrets to Freedom and Success in 5 easy steps*"

Sharon is a member of many professional bodies and associations including Franchise Council of Australia and Women in Franchising.

She lives in Queensland, Australia with her partner John.

RECOMMENDED RESOURCES

Sharon Jurd Events

Sharon Jurd Events offers a unique experience in business growth, bringing like-minded people together to learn, explore and discover their full potential through seminars, motivational materials, webinars, books and consultations on a range of business subjects.

You'll be shown how to identify exactly what to do to maximise your businesses productivity and profits. You'll also receive specific coaching to help you apply the most important strategies to achieve better profits for far less effort.

Sharon Jurd Events seminars have an impressive format unlike any other you have attended including international guest speakers who are successful in their own right, giving you unprecedented insights into their successes and businesses secrets.

You will also have the opportunity to have quality one-on-one time with the presenters who all have a natural 'giving' attitude to help you grow your business fast.

Sharon Jurd Events provides a range of business educational materials including the international best selling book, *How to Grow Your Business Faster than your Competitors*, and inspirational support material all available through the Sharon Jurd Events website.

With over 20 years experience in growing and building successful national businesses, Sharon Jurd Events delivers seminars, business coaching and mentoring in a an impressive and informative format to show you a proven formula to reach financial freedom and success.

If you're serious about growing your business to its fullest potential, Sharon Jurd Events reaches out to 'Impress the Mind and Move the Feelings'.

Sharon Jurd Events
Sharon Jurd
CEO
PO Box 409
Labrador QLD 4215
Australia
0429 686 586
sharonjurd@sharonjurdevents.com.au
www.sharonjurdevents.com.au

HydroKleen Australia

HydroKleen Australia is a master franchisor that has developed the most comprehensive method for cleaning split system air conditioning units, eliminating a range of contaminants that are commonly found, significantly improving the quality of the air, and reducing power consumption.

HydroKleen was founded in 2009 after extensive research found a need for speeding up the process of servicing and cleaning split system air conditioners, especially given that nearly every household has one or more air conditioner of some sort, and there was no industry standard for the servicing and cleaning of air conditioners.

The HydroKleen system can completely wet wash and sanitise an air conditioner with a no splash, no mess result, and allows for ease of use in people's homes with the facility to carry out a pressure wash without damaging property, a major point of difference within the air conditioning industry.

HydroKleen Australia established its national head office on the Gold Coast in 2010 due to its accessibility and strategic position to the north and south of Australia. Since then the company has grown to 19 franchises Australia wide (as of June 2013) employing over 50 people with many more territories in each state currently under application.

HydroKleen franchisees are primarily air conditioning companies who understand a need to add an additional profit centre to their already existing business.

The HydroKleen model is based around an unlicensed technician as a 'man in the van' application and is proving to be overwhelmingly successful for this market.

HydroKleen Australia
John Sanders & Sharon Jurd
Directors
6/12 Tonga Place
Parkwood QLD 4214
Australia
07 557 449 08
service@hydrokleen.com.au
www.hydrokleen.com.au

bartercard

Bartercard Gold Coast

Networking is a great way to build your business and stay ahead of your competition. By building business relationships you develop loyal customers and word of mouth marketers for your business.

Bartercard has been working with business owners for over 22 years to help them connect and provide businesses with a flexible, secure and fully accountable way to transact their goods and services with businesses all around the country and the world without the need for cash.

Bartercard members are able to make more money by reducing expenses in their business using their excess stock or spare capacity to barter with other members and gain extra business from the loyal network.

Like-minded business members are effectively using barter to...
- gain new customers, who generate extra income
- move excess stock or utilise downtime
- free up cash that would otherwise be used to pay existing expenses
- increase profits from the introduction of new business

Bartercard members can cost-effectively expand their business reach by promoting within the network. Bartercard has a nationwide membership of approximately 20,000 Australian businesses, and over 35,000 globally. This provides Bartercard members with strong marketing and trading options through its national and international directory service, plus the online business website where members actively promote their business and conduct business transactions and the mobile phone application.

Visit our website today to see how you can use barter to save cash in your business and connect with business people just like you.

Bartercard Gold Coast
Leigh Watson
Brokerage Manager
Level 1, 121 Scarborough Street
Southport QLD 4215
Australia
07 5561 9999
Leigh.watson@bartercardgldcst.com.au
www.bartercard.com.au

Call2View Real Estate

Call2View Real Estate is an award winning agency that specializes in residential sales and property management.

Our dynamic team is an accomplished group of professionals who are young and vibrant with motivated outcomes. We consistently attain results for our clients with integrity and transparency. We work together to exceed our clients' expectations at all times.

We'll help you find the right property to suit your needs, whether it is a property for your family to call home or an investment property to earn you passive income to secure your future. Our team continually strives to implement innovative marketing strategies and our systems, processes, procedures and policies ensures our team understands your needs are meet every time.

We are dedicated to providing the highest level of service to all buyers, sellers, landlords and tenants. Our aim is to provide Territorians and all Australian & international investors with unparalleled professionalism and personal service with a fulfilling experience in attaining our clients Real Estate goals.

We are committed to being honest, ethical, knowledgeable and caring individuals to ourselves, our clients, our friends and one another.

"Experience is our strength – exceptional service is our priority"

Call2View Real Estate
Jody & Adam Hayes
Directors
9/41 Georgina Crescent
Yarrawonga NT 0830
Australia
08 89328858
jody@call2view.com.au
www.call2view.com.au

Pat Mesiti Pty Ltd

Pat is a self-made multi-millionaire and is an internationally celebrated and gifted speaker, seasoned business executive, entrepreneur, mindset growth strategist, bestselling author and consultant.

Pat's passion is to equip and empower individuals and businesses to experience growth and prosperity to their fullest potential. His expertise is to shift mindsets and to build bigger people to produce results.

His dynamic leadership and business skills have allowed him to build the largest and most successful youth organisation in the southern hemisphere, "Youth Alive" having over 15,000 teens in regular attendance.

Pat also graduated over 400 young Men with drug addictions into a recovery program with a staggering 86% success rate.

Pat's books have sold in excess of 700,000 copies worldwide and his motivational programs have sold over 2 million copies internationally — transforming the lives of all it touches.

He is recognised as an expert in the field of motivation and creating a Millionaire Mindset, business development, executive mentoring, international speaking, self-development, relationships and accelerated mental and emotional transformation.

He is the author of 8 best-selling books such as "The $1 Million Reason to Change Your Mind" "How to Have a Millionaire Mindset", "Soaring Higher", "Dreamers Never Sleep", and "Staying Together Without Falling Apart" just to name a few.

Pat's enthusiasm combined with his great sense of humour gives him the ability to move an audience into action as well as give them practical resources to help them achieve their goals.

Pat is committed to helping raise 10,000 millionaires through his works. He will shift your mindset, touch your heart and increase your wealth.

Pat Mesiti Pty Ltd
Pat Mesiti
Director
Level 2, Suite 8
56 Delhi Road
North Ryde NSW 2117
Australia
02 99996122
info@mesiti.com
www.mesiti.com

Jazz Cleaning

Jazz Cleaning is a "One Stop Cleaning Service"

We are a Queensland company with head office based on the Gold Coast and have been for many years. We are expanding nationally. We understand that time is precious and cannot be taken for granted. Our team will give you the time to enjoy what you love most.

Jazz Cleaning is a one stop cleaning service and covers all forms of cleaning including: Domestic Cleans, One Off Cleans, Medical Centres, Commercial Properties, Builder Cleans, Bond Cleans, Body Corporate Cleans, Oven Cleaning, Fridge Cleaning, Mattress Sanitising & Carpet Steam Cleaning. Whether it is your home, office, business or investment we look after them like they are our own.

Our customers' health is important to us, so our priority is to use Eco cleaning products. We use all of our own equipment to ensure a professional result.

Our customers have great peace of mind knowing all of our staff are police checked, they are also trained through our dedicated cleaning academy. Managers conduct regular spot checks to maintain the service standards from our team. We believe communication between Jazz Cleaning and our clients is paramount, so we have a unique communication system.

Jazz Cleaning has strong Core Values which include:
- Excellence in service quality
- Pride in our work
- Attention to detail
- Trust, honest & integrity.

We feel it's important to give back to the community; we donate free cleaning to women suffering from cancer.

Jazz Cleaning
Elisa Rooney & Peter Korzuch
Directors
Carrara QLD 4211
Australia
0400084487
contactus@jazzcleaning.com.au
www.jazzcleaning.com.au

Bell Partners

Bell Partners has built its reputation as one of Australia's premier boutique accounting & financial advisory firms on the basis of delivering and exceeding our clients expectations. The business model has evolved since its inception in the 1960's by founding principal Donald Bell. A generational change in the late 1990's led to Anthony Bell acquiring the business from his father, with it now in a position of approximately 100 staff across offices in each of the major capital cities, specialising in business consulting, tax advisory, assurance, wealth creation and finance.

We are proud of our business and how we have helped our clients achieve their goals over many years but it is constantly in the forefront of our minds that we cannot rest on our laurels and must continue to innovate. We are proud to act for many successful small business entrepreneurs, up-and-coming talents as well as established home grown businesses. Many of our clients have started with us needing simple individual tax returns and then progressed with our help to operating highly successful businesses in their own right. Our job is to help you get there.

We believe we have the best people working for us in an environment that rewards initiative and strives for success. It is an attitude that keeps us at the leading edge of accounting and related financial service providers.

We are excited about the future and opportunities for success as we ride out of the Global Financial Crisis, as we forge ahead together, sharing in the continued success of growth and change.

Bell Partners
Darren Morris
Managing Director
Level 3, 164 Grey Street
South Brisbane QLD 4101
Australia
1300 235 575 (1300 BELLQLD)
bellqld@bellpartners.com
www.bellpartners.com

Zakazukha Marketing Communications

Zakazukha is an integrated communications consultancy specialising in marketing and public relations to a wide range of industries.

Our strategy is simple – to help you tell your story, which defines who you are – through the press, newsletters, social media, DVD, in fact any communication, medium you care to think of.

Our recommendations are always based on the need to manage and influence a company's products, services, public image and credentials, and in turn as part of the marketing mix help drive sales or achieve better business outcomes.

Zakazukha can also help you define your audience, whether customers, investors, stakeholders or employees, so you know you're speaking with the right people.

Whichever way you choose to tell your story, it needs to be told in a clear, succinct and professional manner, so you're known for who you are and what you do, and ultimately why you're different from your competitors.

Zakazukha works in partnership with a range of other creative and digital agencies for the common goal of helping our clients become better businesses.

Essentially we strive to work closely with companies to become their total outsourced marketing and public relations department.

Zakazukha can provide a range of services to help you tell the best story to the right audience.

This includes:
- Public Relations
- Communication Strategy
- Creative and Design Services
- Social Media
- Investor Communications
- Copywriting and Content Creation
- Community Consultation and Engagement
- Event Management

To see what we do or to contact us visit our website www.zakazukha.com

Zakazukha Marketing Communications
Bruce Nelson
Director
7/89-99 West Burleigh Road
Burleigh Heads QLD 4220
Australia
07 5607 0899
info@zakazukha.com
www.zakazukha.com

ASKcreative

Design

At ASKcreative we assist clients in leading companies who have FMCG (Fast, Moving, Consumer Goods) in many industries including Food & Beverage, Pharmaceutical and Cosmetic industries , to name a few. We help our clients take their idea and bring it to reality.

We believe that our role of being a packaging designer is that the design has to enrich, inform, be truthful, fit in and stand out from your competition in this high turnover industry.

Packaging design is more than a container with pretty graphics it is a message, a medium and a conversation between buyer and seller.

Branding

Branding is more than just a logo or a catchy name; it's the whole process that surrounds the creation of a unique name.

At ASKcreative we can ensure that your Brand works together and consumers can identify all your visual communications. This ensures consistency is kept and recognisable across all mediums

Graphic Design

We can supply the full graphic design service for print or web. Whether that be a logo design, advertising layout for flyers, magazines or attractive graphics to put in your e-newsletter or website.

We can push the boundary even further we can help you with apps for ipads and other tablets or full digital magazines with video and sound.

ASKcreative
Andrea Welsh
Creative Director
Robina QLD 4226
Australia
07 5559 2923
0433 833 197
andrea@askcreative.com.au
www.askcreative.com.au

Australian Institute of Women

**Australia's peak industry body servicing the Women's Market
Research • Education • Advocacy • Engagement**

The Australian Institute Of Women works with business, government
and industry bodies to promote the advancement of market research,
education and best-practice within this key and significant market
sector for Australia.

Through its industry research, educational programs, products and
services, AIOW focuses on providing critical insights and training
programs on SHEmarket philosophies and emerging trends across all
market sectors.

AIOW also offers a range of professional development services through
its Executive Women's Leadership Development programs, state events
and forums, business coaching, SHEecomony case studies, publications
and annual national conference.

AIOW membership is open to executives, professionals, companies, alliances and associations.

Australian Institute of Women

Karen Phillips

CEO

PO Box 8150

GCMC QLD 9726

Australia

07 5504 6055

info@AIOW.com.au

www.austalianinstituteofwomen.com.au

"FINANCIAL & INSURANCE CONSULTANT SERVICES"

Arrow Insurance

Arrow was established in 1999 to provide Insurance and Financial Advice.

The Directors are Steve and Janet Culpitt. Steve has over 30 years experience in the field of financial planning, advice and service. Janet's history is in human resources, staff training, compliance, process and administration.

Steve is a qualified and well respected Financial Adviser and Risk Insurance Specialist in his Industry. He is professionally qualified, compliant with RG146. His qualifications include: Diploma of Financial Planning (DFP) 1, 2, 3, 4 & 5, Margin Lending and SMSF. Janet's role is Administration Manager and the "Rain Maker" for their business, having proved her expertise and natural ability to meet new contacts and develop relationships that result in both new business and continued growth for all parties.

Combine these attributes and you see why we they are specialists in this area and they are dedicated to providing the appropriate solutions for both businesses and individuals.

Arrow's focus is on assisting clients to protect their lifestyles and to grow wealth. They do this by identifying clients ever changing financial goals and objectives, and then offering tailored, strategic solutions. Customer Service and getting to know their clients and forming long lasting relationships are their priority.

Planning is making smart decisions about money and achieving financial goals.

Arrow's wealth coaching helps you create a clear picture of where you are now, where you want to be and then implement strategies and actions to get there, whilst reviewing regularly to make sure you stay on track.

Arrow Insurance
Steve & Janet Culpitt
Directors
PO Box 652
Mudgeeraba QLD 4213
Australia
07 55303 500
info@arrowinsurance.com.au
www.arrowinsurance.com.au

SMALL BUSINESS GRANTS AND ASSISTANCE

There are numerous grants and advisory services available to assist small and growing businesses through federal and state government programs.

Following is a list of these and other resources which may prove helpful.

FEDERAL

AusIndustry

The Australian Government's business unit within the Department of Industry, Innovation, Climate Change, Science, Research and Tertiary Education provides business assistance to support innovation, investment and international competitiveness.

For more information visit www.ausindustry.gov.au/programs/Pages/programs.aspx

GrantsLINK

Makes it easier to find suitable grants from the many government grants that are available. It also helps you find the best source of funding and assists you to complete application forms. Page lists both business and industry grants.

For more information visit http://grants.myregion.gov.au/grant-categories/business-and-industry

Enterprise Connect

Provides comprehensive support to Australian small and medium sized enterprises (SMEs), to help them become more innovative, efficient and competitive. Through Manufacturing Centres and Innovation Centres, a national network of services and support is provided for eligible SMEs to access expert, practical advice and support tailored to their individual firms.

For more information visit www.enterpriseconnect.gov.au/Pages/Home.aspx

GovForms

GovForms is a single entry point for businesses to quickly and conveniently find, manage and complete the forms online with all levels of government - everything from registering for an ABN, applying for licences, to simply paying your rates.

For more information visit australia.gov.au/service/govforms

STATES

Australian Capital Territory

For business grants, funding, advice and support in the ACT visit www.business.act.gov.au/grants-and-assistance

New South Wales

For people starting, running or growing a small business in NSW visit www.smallbiz.nsw.gov.au

Northern Territory

For support and advice to those who want to start, expand or buy a business in the NT visit www.dob.nt.gov.au

Queensland

For support, tolls and grants in Queensland visit www.business.qld.gov.au/business/support-tools-grants

South Australia

For information to assist South Australian businesses plan and grow their business ideas visit www.dmitre.sa.gov.au/small_business_home

Tasmania

For business grants, funding, advice and support in Tasmania visit www.business.tas.gov.au

Victoria

For financial support, advice, or education and training programs in Victoria visit www.business.vic.gov.au/grants-and-assistance

Western Australia

For grants and programs available to small businesses in Western Australia visit www.smallbusiness.wa.gov.au/grants-and-assistance-available